AN ALTAR IN THE WILDERNESS

AN ALTAR

in the

WILDERNESS

KALEEG HAINSWORTH

RMB

Rocky Mountain Books
www.rmbooks.com

Library and Archives Canada Cataloguing in Publication

Hainsworth, Kaleeg, author
    An altar in the wilderness / Kaleeg Hainsworth.

Includes bibliographical references.
Issued in print and electronic formats.
ISBN 978-1-77160-036-1 (bound).—ISBN 978-1-77160-037-8 (html).—
ISBN 978-1-77160-038-5 (pdf)

    1. Human ecology—Religious aspects. 2. Environmentalism—Religious aspects.
3. Philosophy of nature. I. Title.

GF80.H34 2014   201'.77   C2014-904031-8
                                            C2014-904032-6

Printed in Canada

Rocky Mountain Books acknowledges the financial support for its publishing program from the Government of Canada through the Canada Book Fund (CBF) and the Canada Council for the Arts, and from the province of British Columbia through the British Columbia Arts Council and the Book Publishing Tax Credit.

 Canadian Heritage Patrimoine canadien   Canada Council for the Arts Conseil des Arts du Canada

 BRITISH COLUMBIA ARTS COUNCIL
Supported by the Province of British Columbia

The interior pages of this book have been produced on 100% post-consumer recycled paper, processed chlorine free and printed with vegetable-based dyes.

 FSC
www.fsc.org

MIX
Paper from
responsible sources
FSC® C016245

For Ella, Heulwen and Bridget

*"And in all the land were no women found
so fair as the daughters of Job."*

—Job 42:15

CONTENTS

of Twelve – into the wilderness for seminars on just the subjects I discuss here. I owe each member of that group enormous gratitude and confess that much of their insight and many of the experiences they provided stand behind every page. I'm the kind of man that is blessed with many faithful friends, many of whom have hiked with me and will smile, I'm sure, when they see how many of the things we discussed on the trail have found their way to these chapters. The Stobbes, Bugslags, Wetherells, Schroedels, Jordans, as well as Ginnoula, Andrew, Charles, James, Vera, Andrea, Jean-Claude, Ambrose, Heidi, Akeiko, Muryn, Gabe and Kelsey and many others have taught me the meaning of friendship. I am especially grateful to Matt Root, who read each of these chapters closely and never failed to encourage me in the process. I am filled with thanksgiving for the many brother clergy who have shaped me, both as mentors and as friends: Frs. Hopko, Behr, Francis, Raffan, Skidmore, Koblosh, Baxter, Scratch, Papazian, Maitland-Muir, Archbishop Seraphim and many more whom I love. I owe the entire RMB team, and Don Gorman in particular, enormous gratitude for their support, patience and encouragement throughout the writing of this manifesto. My best friend, Deacon Kevin Miller, used to tell me weekly that every good work I do, no matter how small or big, was being cheered on by God, the angels, the saints, my friends and all of creation. However, when it felt as though the cheers fell silent, it was always his voice that I heard and the only one I needed to hear. "Greater love has no man than this, that he would give his life for his friend" (John 15:13). You are my friend, Kevin. Finally, there is Deborah – poet, punk, activist, visionary, lover of nature, courageous mind, gardener, author, mother (the fabulous kind) – the midwife to this book.

K.H.

Father's Day, 2014

Wells Gray Provincial Park, BC

third-person pronoun has not been found to avoid assigning a male or female gender to God. It is possible to say Him/Her in every instance, but this is hardly an appealing prospect. Using the word "it" is problematic in that such a word does not allow for a personal deity. In this manifesto I have chosen to use "He," with the hope that the reader will understand that in English we are required to use a gender-specific pronoun and that in doing so I am not suggesting that God is male in any way. I have also made careful choices about the examples and imagery I use to illuminate the spiritual ecology outlined in this manifesto, some of which are specifically drawn from the Judeo-Christian tradition. Again, I am not insisting that these be received whole cloth with the traditions that surround them. They are offered here partly as prototypical images that have historic resonance in the human psyche and, as such, reveal profound insights into spirituality and nature. I have been like the honeybee all my life, gathering the nectars from every flower in the spiritual meadows. This book is a honeycomb of pages based on 40 years of reflection and experience in the wilderness and not a Christian apology for nature, and certainly not a manual of belief. I am inviting you on a journey with me and hope that you are challenged to find deeper resonance in your own beliefs about nature. Before we take that journey together, there are three things I want you to know about me because each of these deeply inform this manifesto.

Poet

The first is that I have loved poetry for almost my whole life and it permeates everything I do and say. A poem is a celebration of truth in words. A poet, therefore, must be someone who is devoted to the truth, to the seeing of things as they really are. This is a fundamental devotion that requires courage and self-discipline, because it is somehow human nature to turn our gaze away from the way things are and to fabricate something utterly different. In this way, a poet practises daily the discipline of seeing purely.

A poet must also say purely, however, by which I mean that the words chosen to express what is seen must be exact: the right word used in the right place and in the right relationship with the other words in the poem. No word must be out of place or extraneous. The integrity of the seeing must be matched by the saying. So, in addition to being a lover of the truth, a poet is a lover of words. "There they were, seemingly lifeless, made only of black and white," wrote Dylan Thomas about words, "but out of them, out of their own being, came love and terror and pity and pain and wonder and all the other vague abstractions that make our ephemeral lives dangerous, great and bearable."[1]

Words are wondrous because they are vocalized breath, and breath is the spirit of life. My lifelong love of poetry has taught me that the poet's vocation is fundamental to life on this earth, and therefore in the natural world to which we genetically belong: namely, a fidelity to the truth (however hard it may be to find), and a devotion to the honest use of our breath to vocalize meaning, an art that humans uniquely (and I would add divinely) possess. When we speak about ecology merely as a web of systems and things and evolutionary processes, we miss the point. A rainbow is an arc of colours formed in the sky by the refraction and dispersion of the sun's light by water droplets in the atmosphere. This is what it is. But that's not what it means. Spiritual ecology, such as I plan to introduce to you here, needs the poet.

Priest

The second fact about your author is that I am an Eastern Orthodox priest. The Orthodox Church, with 250 million members, is the second-largest Christian communion and shared the first thousand years of Christian history with the Roman Catholic Church until the schism in the 11th century. Most eastern countries, such as Russia, Greece, Ukraine, the Middle East, Romania, Turkey and Egypt, are culturally Orthodox (or were for hundreds of years before the rise of Islam), and even some of the First Nations in Alaska (the Aleut and Tlingit, for instance) consider Eastern Orthodoxy their native religion.

My own journey to the Orthodox Church was somewhat anomalous. I grew up in a secular household with no religious affiliation, but I felt a divine calling from a very young age and spent a good deal of my early life searching for its source. In 1992 I had a conversion experience that led me to call the Orthodox Church my home. I was ordained in 2002 after studying for three years at an Orthodox theological seminary in New York and thereafter served as a parish priest for ten years in Victoria, BC. You will notice that this book draws from the resources of many spiritual traditions, including a great deal from my own, gathered from years of reading in, and practising, the spiritual life. The richness of Orthodox spirituality on the subject of ecology is vast but almost unknown in the West. The Eastern Orthodox world view has not been shaped by Western history and dialogues; we rarely polarize faith and science, and our rituals and traditions are rooted in the earth, the cycles of natural life and, most of all, in beauty.

This ecological manifesto bears a lot of my experience of the priesthood. I have seen first-hand the transformational power of an ecologically minded practice in the spiritual lives of many. What is more, I have learned a good deal, mostly through trial and error (and mostly still through error), about the geography of the spiritual life through my years as a priest working within (though not exclusively) my tradition and serving others. It is my conviction, which I will of course explain, that each of us is a priest to the natural world and that each of us, in our own way, must become (or build!) an altar in the wilderness, a place of offering and sacrifice, a place of healing and reconciliation.

Father

The third fact about me is that I am a single dad raising three daughters full time. I consider this to be my highest vocation, and it has taught me several things that also form part of the foundation to this manifesto. One of the key lessons can be summed up neatly this way: "God can bring great beauty out of complete devastation." This is a saying of Olga Michael, a Yup'ik woman who is widely venerated among the First Nations in Alaska as a saint.[2] In 2009 my marriage of 15 years began to disintegrate, and the rest of what I had built in my life along with it. In a short amount of time I lost my home, car, books, possessions, all my savings and, most frighteningly, my identity. Worst of all, there was nothing I could do to stop it all from happening. The story arc of the first 40 years of my life changed dramatically and I felt as though I was left without a story. This was the "complete devastation" part. However, looking back now, I see that my marriage was unsustainable and so was how I was living my life. The story had to change.

I think that the human paradigm we are living today is also an unsustainable story. Ecosystem devastation, species extinction, unchecked re-source extraction, wasteful consumerism and ex-ploding population growth are leading to changes not only in the availability of clean air and essen-tials such as food and water for all, but also in the integrity of the planet's basic systems on which all life depends. These factors alone will alter almost everything we expect from modern life in the West. Disillusion of any kind is a healthy, though painful, process, so this inevitability actually gives me hope. This is what my experience of becoming a single father has taught me. Finding a new story and a more natural way of living, one that takes into account who we are and what our place is in the natural world, will be the great beauty that emerges from the devastation.

What my daughters have taught me, how-ever, is much more important. This is wonder. My girls have spent much of their life following me on hikes all over the world. In some cases, this has demanded from them extraordinary strength and courage – being caught in the backcountry at night and having to find our way to safety through the darkness, or scampering around cliff faces, or trudging for kilometres through rain-soaked, muddy forests. My daughters will carry the memories of these experiences all their lives, and I'm sure they will be shaped by them.

Children need to be challenged in nature and at the very least be exposed to it often. The adventure inherent in experiencing the outdoors cultivates attachment to it, leading to engagement and, ultimately, love and appreciation. Most of all, though, when a young person experiences outdoor adventures, it calls out the natural sense of wonder in them. This wonder is a very active kind; I would describe it as playful. Recently, I hiked a long, gruelling trail straight up a mountain face with a small group of teens from a youth camp. When we arrived at the top, a turquoise-blue alpine lake cradled by three snowy mountain peaks greeted us. The teens stopped in their tracks before the majesty before them, silent. They stared for a moment, taking everything in. Then one said to the others, "Let's go!" They were off like a shot, leaping over logs, wading through the cold waters, skipping rocks, searching for fish and tadpoles or whatever they could find. This is what wonder is, and this, for me, is the gateway to an authentic spiritual ecology.

So poetry, spirituality, faith, priesthood, fatherhood, seeing and speaking the truth in love, an appreciation of nature and a wonder that leads to play – these are the things I bring personally to the forthcoming pages. My hope is that these things, as well as the observations I offer you from a lifetime of reflection on God and nature, will lead you into the wilderness our souls share with the astounding complexity of the natural world, and show you why building your own altar – inside or out – is vital to healing the deep divisions between human beings and nature that now, as never before, are becoming manifest.

INTRODUCTION

In this book, I am inviting you on a journey into the wilderness with me where I will ask you to build an altar and there make an offering. Whenever I head out into the wilderness, I make sure that I know where I'm going and have everything I need for the trek. Our ultimate destination is the heart, where I believe we build our altar. To get there, however, we will need to explore our cosmos. Chapter One is all about this. What is creation? What does it express about its creator and about us as human beings? I want to get right into the freshness where I believe, like the poet Gerard Manley Hopkins, whom I will discuss later in the book, dwell "deep down things." This is the journey into the wilderness itself.

Once there, we will want to enjoy the scenery. Chapter Two is a study of beauty, the role of beauty in our world and how we experience it and its effects on us when we do. The natural world reveals the beauty of the divine nature that fills it. Yet it also reveals another wilderness, that of the human being. Chapter Three explores the relationship between these two wildernesses and shows how much the one affects the other. I will introduce you to the wilderness temple and what it offers those of us who visit it. In Chapter Four, "With the drawing of this Love and the voice of this Calling," as T.S. Eliot wrote in "Little Gidding" in *Four Quartets*, "We shall not cease from exploration / And the end of all our exploring / Will be to arrive where we started / And know the place for the first time."[3] The power of our hearts to transform the world around us is tremendous. I will propose that we build our altars there and offer to God, on behalf of creation, a sacrifice of ourselves in a spirit of thanksgiving. Finally, in the Postscript, I offer one among many tools that we may use to heal the human/nature divide. I sincerely believe that this journey of ours will save the world.

So what's in our pack? Many things, really, but there are a few items that are essential for this trip into the world of spiritual ecology. First of all, we only because it is customary for a priest to dress this way in my church tradition but also because I knew that I was immediately identifiable as a priest to the inmates. Most of the older inmates knew exactly how to address me and rarely had questions, though they almost always had requests for prayers or blessings. The younger ones, however, looked on me with curiosity and caution ("Here comes Blackrobe," I remember one announcing) and often approached me with a challenge of one kind or another, which I always welcomed.

During one visit, a young inmate started a conversation by saying, with a tone of defiance, "Hey, father, I consider myself a spiritual man, not a religious one." He had no idea that I had heard that phrase – spiritual, not religious – so often that it felt to me like a well-worn cliché. I replied immediately, "Good! I'm not a religious man either!" The inmate looked surprised; I could see the wheels spinning behind his eyes. I explained that religion is a set of beliefs and practices that govern a relationship between human beings and the god or gods they worship. The underlying presupposition here is a separation between humans and the gods, one that needs laws and practices to hold together, like a separation agreement between two estranged, divorcing parties.

I explained that my own experience of faith and church life (in the Eastern Orthodox Christian tradition) is that life with God was no more a religion, in this context, than a marriage. Certainly there is a covenant between two married people, a binding agreement to live together, but the practices and customs within that marriage are simply the day-to-day expressions of a life lived in union. The experience of most people engaged in faith traditions around the world is largely the same, namely a rich relationship with the divine in which rituals emerge from within the relationship rather than being imposed from an outside source in order to govern it. When I had said all of this to the inmate, he thought for a moment and replied, "Hm. All sounds like a lot of work. I'm happier divorced!"

The truth is that people today tend to create a false dichotomy between spirituality and religion, the same way we started to separate science from religion at the beginning of the Industrial Revolution. What I usually hear (in order of frequency) is that religion is 1) responsible for too many wars; 2) out of touch with modern life; 3) too exclusive and intolerant of other faiths; 4) too full of rules; 5) prone to reject alternative lifestyles; 6) hierarchical; 7) favours men over women; 8) an opiate for the masses and 9) in opposition to the purity of nature. There is a grain of truth in each of these statements, as anyone honestly engaged in their faith tradition will aver, but experience has taught me that too often these are platitudes that deflect attention from what is really being expressed, which is "I want a spiritual life on my own terms."

The prevailing desire is to assemble a set of beliefs, informally, of course, that are gathered from any spiritual resource regardless of context; that make no unreasonable demands on how we want to live; that are accepting of all peoples and faiths, though obviously rejecting faith traditions that make exclusive claims about God; and that ultimately make us feel better about ourselves. Yet such an approach, in my opinion, does not arrive at a spiritual life at all. If there is one thing the saints and holy people of every faith tradition agree on, it is that the spiritual life begins only when we have set aside our own terms and conditions. I have never found a story or example in recorded history of a person embarking on a spiritual journey and finding that it was exactly what he or she expected.

On the contrary, the journey is a harrowing experience, "costing," in T.S. Eliot's words, "not less than everything,"[5] and when the divine is encountered, everything changes again. In story after story, whether historical or mythical or in between, we find one simple axiom: a god in our own image is not God. It might be more convenient to shape God in our image, but any authentic encounter with the divine actually shapes us.

Spirituality is hard because it demands that we question everything we think we know on a daily basis, whether we hold to the teachings of a particular faith tradition or not. But it is also hard because it requires discipline, vigilance, humility, love, patience and gratitude. Tall order, I know. Luckily, spirituality does not require success. There is an apocryphal story about a pilgrim who made a journey to one of the desert monks in Egypt. He asked him, "What is the monk's life like?" The spiritual master replied, "We fall down, we get up. We fall down, and we get up again. We do this every day." It's the getting up part that I know from experience to be the most difficult.

However, let's address the falling down part first, since it raises one very important question: Fall down from what? The answer, unequivocally, is love. I do not mean romantic love, which is as changeable and unpredictable as the weather. I mean the love that "bears all things, believes all things, hopes all things, endures all things" (1 Cor. 13:7). Some in the Greek world called this love *agape*, the highest of the four loves – *storge* (familial love), *eros* (romantic, erotic) and *philia* (friendship) being the other three in ascending order.[6] This agapic love was, in fact, rarely discussed in ancient Greek culture, despite having a category for it, because it was very difficult to attain and express and was thus perceived as somewhat impractical.[7]

However, when the early Christians needed a word to express divine love as they saw it expressed in Christ's sacrifice on the cross, they readily chose agape for its unconditional, universal and divine qualities. The same love is expressed in Buddhist teachings, where it is classified as freedom. All love that inspires freedom from passions, from lust, from neediness, and which does not require the love of another in response, is considered the highest state of spiritual freedom for the Buddhist. Every other virtue – humility, patience, peace, kindness etc. – is the fruit of this kind of love, which is the branch and root of life. This is one reason why, in the Genesis story, the eating of the forbidden fruit in the garden was such a serious act of treason: it was an act against the agapic love of God in favour of self-love, since it was self-referential and utterly self-directed.

My experience as a priest and confessor has taught me two things about this love and its specific application to the spiritual life. First, it is very easy to talk about in wonderful ways as long as it remains in the abstract. And people do so ad nauseam. But when actually applied to other people and our environment, this love becomes our hardest, most demanding undertaking, and we realize why it is the highest of the loves and the foundation to any authentic spirituality. But, secondly, I have learned that there are two kinds of human responses to the manifestation of unconditional, free and agapic love. We either take it for granted, or we simply can't conceive of it and therefore either reject it or test it. In the case of the latter, we want to prove that all love has limits and will ultimately fail us, whether because we have been abandoned or have experienced trauma as young children, or because all we have ever known is human love, which always has limits and conditions. Either way, when we cannot love as God loves, or shy away from it for whatever reason we may have, we fall down.

The getting up again, however, is exactly what comprises the spiritual life. At first it appears easier to stay down. We might feel shame, guilt or despair, all very heavy forces indeed, and sometimes just getting up in the morning is more daunting than we have the strength for. But here we have to ask ourselves, Whose ideals are we supposed to get up for? Whose expectations are we trying to live up to? Usually they're our own or someone else's. Our main focus in getting up again must instead be the truth that we are loved; that we are capable of love; and that all our errors of judgment, our pains and aches in life, exist within the boundless and unconditional love that some call God, others freedom, others the universe, but which all faith traditions and experienced holy people proclaim as existing. Certainly, we must address seriously and take ownership of what we do. This is called being responsible for our actions, and learning why we fell to begin with helps us learn how not to fall again. But rising again to receive and emulate the love of God means that we leave our burdens on the ground around us. "The angels can fly," as G.K. Chesterton quipped, "because they can take themselves lightly."[8]

So the spiritual life is about love, rising to it again when we fall or are hurt, seeking to embody through our experience of it the virtues it inspires: forgiveness, patience, honesty, freedom, empathy, strength. To embody this love, we must be willing to endure the experience of having our core beliefs challenged, especially if we adhere to any specific faith tradition. Spirituality is not for hobbyists. We engage with the spiritual world every time we reach beyond ourselves, every time we encounter and form relationships with other people. This is why it is so worthwhile to explore what our spiritual approach to the environment looks like, because however we got here, we belong to a complex, plenitudinous ecosystem that extends beyond us limitlessly in all directions. If it's possible to say that spirituality begins the moment we enter into a relationship (with God, with each other, with our pet, with a garden), then how great is the need for spiritual ecology? We are, after all, in a relationship with every living thing on this planet, even if we can't see so far as to know it.

Sacrament and Ecology

The first time I realized that the universe had something to say to me, I was 12 years old and hiking in the Kananaskis region of the Rocky Mountains. My family and I had spent a long weekend trekking to a remote lake high in the alpine, reached only by a steep shale traverse up a mountain pass. The pass presented itself only at the end of an already long day of hiking and climbing it seemed to take *forever*. When the trail levelled, however, and the view opened, my eyes widened at the sight waiting for us. An alpine meadow stretched as far as I could see, flanked by two snowy peaks and crammed with red paintbrushes, purple crocuses, blue forget-me-nots and shooting stars. The wildflowers were bright with sun under a wide blue sky and swaying this way and that in the haphazard breezes from the slopes. There are moments in life that are different from any other; they seem fixed in time and history, like waypoints in a journey.

We arrive at them without warning, stumbling, and depart a different person with new purpose, with transformed vision and self-revelation. I had seen such beauty before, but in this moment I suddenly felt like Keats's "Watcher of the skies / When a new planet swims into his ken."[9]

What I had stumbled into as a dorky pre-teen boy was indeed a new planet, not a different one, but I saw this planet through eyes of wonder and awe. I remembered a quote I saw on a greeting card as a boy that claimed, "If we would see this world as the angels do, we would be ravished and enraptured as the angels are." I was seeing like his angels and wondering how I could have missed until now the radiant inner world around me. I say inner world, but perhaps inter-world would be a better spatial designation. This world, of which I had known only the natural part until now, was as much a revelation of individual elements as one of a complex network of relatedness. Each flower seemed to proclaim itself, but in relation to all the other flowers and the scenery in general. Everything around me was communicating and I felt invited to join the conversation. "It is a blessed thing," observed John Muir, "to go free in the light of this beautiful world, to see God playing upon everything as on an instrument, His fingers upon the lightning and torrent, on every wave of sea and sky, and every living thing, making all together sing and shine in sweet accord, the one love-harmony of the Universe."[10]

This "see[ing] God playing upon everything as on an instrument" is essentially seeing the world as sacramental and is vital to spiritual ecology. I know well that the word "sacrament" is most often associated with Christianity and it certainly has a lot of baggage that goes with it. But spiritual ecology, indeed spirituality in general, is nothing without it. Simply put, a sacrament is something that reveals the sacred. The alpine flowers I witnessed in the Kananaskis were a sacrament, as was the wind in that valley. Perhaps to the flowers and the wind I was a sacrament too. Everything was communicating something of itself, and that something was inherently sacred.

The key message here is that nature is communicating constantly. The genius of Indigenous spirituality is that it understands this and listens. The "voices" of the great bear or the caribou, the salmon or the eagle, are vitally important to survival;

indeed, these voices speak to us and can even help reveal our identities to us. In Eric Collier's classic memoir *Three Against the Wilderness*, about being a pioneering family in the Chilcotin region of British Columbia, there is a description of a wise old First Nations woman with whom he converses about where to settle and how. In this wonderful piece of reportage, we have a first-hand picture of the kind of wisdom these Native peoples, so much a part of the land, possess:

> Tucked away within the recesses of Lala's wise old mind was a veritable storehouse of knowledge concerning the land as it was when the white man first came to it. Though she knew nothing of biology as printed in any book, the everyday chores of an era when she and the others of her tribe were entirely reliant upon the wildlife resources of the land had brought her into almost daily contact with the complex laws of Nature. Lala knew well of the seven kind years and the seven lean years, and her knowledge was not gleaned from a Bible. The interplay of the cycles that have such paramount bearing upon

> the fortunes of all wildlife communities was
> as familiar to Lala as the letters of the alpha-
> bet to a child of civilization. If Lala's biologi-
> cal knowledge came to her from the campus
> of the wilderness itself, she could not perhaps
> have attended a better school of learning.[11]

I wish the churches would listen more to this kind of spirituality. Indeed, I wish the churches would listen more in general! Father Alexander Schmemann, a well-known Russian theologian, asked in one of his journals, "what is there to talk about so much in Christianity, and what for?"[12] What colonial spirituality needs to learn (among other things) from the faith traditions of the First Nations is simply this: stop telling people things and listen to what the natural world is telling us. Theirs is a journey from a human isolation to a harmony with the natural world. I have always picked up a sense from their stories and rituals that it is nature, and not humans, that is the real authority. It speaks to us, and if we listen, we thrive; if we do not, we die. One thing is clear: listening is love in action. We must love the world God created and lean in to hear his voice in it.

I recently overheard a revealing conversation between a young engineer and an older builder/contractor at the racquet club where I play squash. They had just finished their game and were chatting within my earshot outside the court. The older man asked what the other's summer plans were. The engineer replied that he was heading into the interior of British Columbia to work on a new dam. The older man offered congratulations to the engineer on his first major gig since graduating from engineering school at university. The engineer, however, was more reserved. He said he had visited the place where they were going to build the dam and he was struck by the beauty of the valleys and forests that would soon be submerged by the new lake he would help to create. The other man was dismissive in his reply, telling him this was a necessary loss for progress, adding that "there are too many wacky environmentalists getting in the way anyway." But the engineer had more to say. He agreed the dam needed to be built to meet the power needs of British Columbians and the Americans who would be buying some of the power generated by it. But he returned again to how beautiful this valley actually was. He spoke as its beauty. There may be more nice valleys, but none are *this* nice valley.

In fact, *this* nice valley is the only one of its kind in the universe. We have developed powerful defence mechanisms against, and justifications to subdue, our impulse to listen to the sacred in our world. But it is naive to think that beauty is a luxury we can really afford to sacrifice for energy. What if this engineer followed his heart into the beauty speaking to him from the valley? Remember how Native spirituality listens to nature as a course of survival? It is very reasonable to say that if he had followed it, he might have found other ways to generate power or perhaps discovered a reason why the valley was crucial to the ecosystems around it. Who knows? But listening to the voice calling us to deeper engagement in any course of life is always better than the defences and justifications we throw up to ignore it. I'm not saying don't build dams, and I, like anyone, support jobs and revenue. I'm saying that the whole thrust of modern Western life ignores, and is manufactured to ignore, spiritual ecology with its sacramental vision. I'm saying that we are so inoculated to the sacred voices of nature that we consider them either imaginary or irrelevant or both. And finally, I'm saying that listening will certainly make us vulnerable to change, but what we hear will only benefit us in the long run.

The Hungry Bear

Our ecological world view must also answer to the realities of nature. After all, nature itself is very harsh. A hungry bear, with no other options, will attack and eat us without remorse or second thought for our families and friends. The animals themselves do not live easy lives; they almost always meet their end either in the jaws of another animal or through starvation or disease. One trapper told me he once watched a moose become so tortured by clouds of flies and mosquitos that it grew disoriented and fell off a rock face. He had to put the injured moose down himself and then butchered it for the meat. A park ranger in British Columbia's Manning Park told me he watched with horror as two crows bullied a loon to the point of chasing it down and killing it. They then proceeded to dismember it for no apparent reason. "Nature," said Alfred Lord Tennyson, is "red in tooth and claw."[13] Certainly we humans have adapted so well to our environment that in many cities we are insulated for the most part against weather systems, predators, dangerous terrain and hunger. This fact makes it extremely tempting to write about nature with detachment and pieties, devoid of any real-world application beyond the city garden or rural hobby farm.

I am advocating not just for a spiritual ecology but also an experienced one. There is simply no substitute for getting out into the wild, where we discover immediately that pious descriptions about the harmony and beauty of nature don't help us survive. We also discover a very different human modality. For instance, in the ecosystems most of us are used to, we have level streets, laid out in grids that allow us to move through our world with ease, speed and safety. When I go into the backcountry, the first adjustment I have to make is to regain my balance, my "bush balance," I call it. The paths and terrain are not level; there are obstacles like fallen trees, roots, rocks and mud-holes. Also, I have to navigate differently. There are no street signs, right angles or traffic rules. I am forced to look at my surroundings – the mountains around me, the position of the sun in the sky, the changing vegetation – in order to determine my direction. Getting to and from a destination without the mediation of signs and grids requires a wholly different set of skills and even instinct. Suddenly I am paying attention to elevation, vegetation, wind direction, constellations and topography, and I am in direct communication with nature, involving more of my senses than I would in the city.

I am not suggesting we abandon streets and sidewalks. I wonder, however, whether we have taken in how different these two ways of moving in the world are and whether we have fully grasped their impact on our daily life. Being confined to a grid, and only moving over level ground without obstacles of any kind, affects our psyches in a radically different way than being in vast, trackless, open spaces, moving over rough terrain (not to mention differences in light sources, food preparation and preservation and clothing needs). When all these things are taken together, we can see that modern life is substantially different for us as a species now than it has been for most of our ancestors.

This gives me pause for two reasons. First, we have no idea what kind of impacts our new, manufactured ecosystem is having on us in the long term. We know, for instance, that fundamental changes in movement over the earth (grids, streets, cars) have contributed to high levels of obesity, which in turn affect our health and the healthcare system. Jerry Mander, in his modern classic, *Four Arguments for the Elimination of Television*, considers the neurophysiological impact artificial light has had on human culture. He says we simply don't have enough data yet to understand these impacts. Today we are subjected to street lights, store lights, car lights, ceiling lights, lamp lights and of course the omnipresent screens. This leads to further alienation from the natural circadian rhythms of night and day that have shaped human life down to the genetic level, and further isolates us within our artificial ecosystem. If the fundamentals of movement and illumination have had such a dramatic impact, what about the myriad other innovations that buttress modern life? Plastic? Digital communication? Food engineering? What we do know, and I think every one of us is unsettled by the knowledge of it, is that life as we live it today bears almost no resemblance to life as our ancestors lived it for tens of thousands of years.

But on the other hand, I realized that I was packing as if I were going to a foreign world, one in which I did not fundamentally belong. I felt as though I were a deep-sea diver, wearing my pack like an air tank, going into some inhospitable place where I could only survive for so long before coming up for air again in my natural city environment. We live most of our lives in a petroleum bubble, sheltered in almost every way from raw nature. I happen to like my place in this bubble – it's comfortable and I like comfort – and I can't see any way to leave it, at least for now. But it does reveal, especially when we leave it and take as much from it as we can carry, just how alienated we have become from the world of nature. I asked myself if I could survive outside the bubble if I took nothing with me. After all, my ancestors survived before the modern world, as did the peoples of the First Nations. Having spent a lifetime hiking and exploring my mountain regions, I really only know of a handful of wild berries and plants that I can eat. I have no knowledge of hunting without a gun, and little idea about how to construct a semi-permanent shelter. I have become institutionalized in the city.

Here arises my second and larger concern, namely that our artificial environment deprives us of a direct knowledge of nature. Most people today know more about their computer operating system than they do about the trees and birds outside their windows. How many of us could name even a handful of the tree, plant, flower and bird species we walk past every day to work or school? And yet I'll wager most of us could name, and speak at length, about almost every mobile phone and car we see on the same journey. What do we know anymore about the stars and constellations, about growing food, about the migration patterns of birds and animals, about the salmon runs, about the natural trades, like the hewing and shaping of wood, or about the subtleties of seasonal change, wind direction, cloud formation and the tides? This used to be the common inheritance of humankind, but now it exists mostly in the domain of naturalists, scientists and people we consider to be living dangerously close to the fringe of modern society.

This lack of direct knowledge of nature is a serious loss for humanity, one that Jane Jacobs, in her final work, *Dark Age Ahead*, identified, as the title of the book suggests, as one of the signs of a new age of fatal ignorance. It also leads to an ecological world view that is either too cerebral (romantic or illusory) or materialistic (the world is mine to exploit and reshape to my purpose). This, for me, is why there is no substitute for experiencing the raw realities of the natural world with all its immensity, intricacy, ferocity and beauty. We must even, from time to time, break out of our artificial ecosystem, cozy and amusing as it is, and engage with the environment we belong in and to. When we do so, we recover the sacredness of nature, but not before.

With these three things in mind – the basics of the spiritual life, a sacramental vision and a grounded approach to nature – we are able to take our first steps toward the altar in the wilderness and there is no better place to begin than in the beginning: the origin and nature of the cosmos.

the evolutionary science we know today it appears painfully naive, hardly possible to take seriously. When I served as a university chaplain, Judeo-Christian students with a dilemma sometimes approached me. They had grown up with this story, but in university they were encountering a much more sophisticated and plausible version of how life on earth evolved. They felt that to accept the evolutionary model was not only to reject the Genesis story but also the faith and family that came with it. This is an unnecessary dilemma, for the Genesis story is not science and it is not meant to be read as history; it is an ancient story drawn from many sources in prehistoric Mesopotamia and is a distillation of many profound observations of human nature, life on earth and spiritual ecology.

I have been asked why, if we have so much knowledge now, we would read such an ancient text as Genesis at all. The answer is simple: the sum of all we know and could know about the origin of the universe or life on earth will only answer *what* happened and maybe *how*. The Large Hadron Collider, for instance, might reveal the so-called God particle, but it will never tell us why it exists in the first place. Genesis, like all great has been introduced here – there is a beginning, here it is and in this beginning God did something. But what is actually being said is that "God, who is the beginning, created heaven and earth." In other words, God is the first principle for everything that comes into existence. If there was a Big Bang, then God lit the fuse. Everything that came from that Big Bang, from particles to galaxies to the physical laws that govern them, also bears in some way the divine mind from which it came. So, to say "God, who is the beginning" is to say that God not only stands at the beginning before time and creation but also that He is the principle through which everything is formed. In the fourth gospel of the New Testament, John has the chutzpah to adjust the text of Genesis in light of his belief in Jesus as the promised Messiah. He says, "In the beginning was the Word," meaning that Jesus was with God before all things (John 1:1). His choice of "word" is significant (the Greek word John uses is *logos*, which has a long history in Greek philosophy and psychology) because by it he is saying, essentially, that God is the word and creation is the language. To put it another way, God is the deep structure from which all things take their shape, meaning and substance – an endless cornucopian diversity tumbling out from a living singularity.

The narrative of Genesis continues as God brings from Himself light, the stars, the sun and moon, the seas and land, the birds, animals and fish, the plants and flowers and, finally, the human being. But what is truly wonderful about this text for me is the sixfold declaration that it is all "good." At the end of each day of creation, we hear, "And God saw that it was good" (Gen. 1:4, 1:10, 1:12, 1:18, 1:21, 1:25, 1:31). It would be understandable if we glossed over this, because "good" has a very broad semantic range in English. In this text, however, it is a powerful statement about God and what He is doing. The ancient Greek version of Genesis (the Septuagint of the first century BC) uses the word *kalos*, which means beautiful, upright, motivating, correct, God-bearing, full, according to principle and much more. In other words, God beholds the cosmos taking shape and declares it to be beautiful. And He does so *six* times. In fact, each thing created is beautiful; I would like to be even more specific and say that each thing created is the divinely embodied word for beautiful.

God speaks, His language is creation and

everything created is the word "beauty." We will come back to beauty, and why it is so important, in the next chapter. However, it is worth meditating on this, since it has profound consequences for how we view ourselves and nature. For instance, if I am a creation of God, then I am God's word for beautiful. I am also created correct, life-bearing, creative and self-revealing of the creator. This means you are too, as is everything we see and know in life. God, who is the beginning, created everything, and everything is an expression of beauty and goodness. Everything, therefore, is god-bearing.

Several years ago, two of my daughters were quietly eating cereal with me at the kitchen table. The younger looked up and asked her sister, "Ella, what's life?" Her sister, 7 years old at the time, thought for a moment and replied, "Life is being, created by God." I knew right away what she meant. We had just been speaking the night before about life as a constantly unfolding creation. Her sister, however, was not as impressed: "No, Ella, I mean what is Life cereal?"

Despite this small misunderstanding, Ella's first response was right on the money. In a wonderful little book called *Theology of Wonder*, Seraphim

Sigrist recounts hearing a rabbinic scholar remark that for God, the act of creation and the act of sustaining are one act, meaning that God creates every moment anew. We draw each new breath from a wholly new creation. The great ecologist John Muir similarly described the continuous unfolding of creation this way in his journal of summer, 1879:

> One learns that the world, though made, is yet being made; that this is still the morning of creation; that mountains and valleys long conceived are now being born, channels traced for coming rivers, basins hollowed for lakes; that moraine soil is being ground and outspread for coming plants ... building particle on particle, cementing and crystallizing, to make the mountains and valleys and plains ... which like fluent, pulsing water, rise and fall and pass on through the ages in endless rhythm and beauty.[15]

Another way to understand this is offered by a seventh-century Byzantine genius named Maximus. He was great at asking good questions and had the ability to answer them in ways that both synthesized and transformed the philosophical and theological traditions that preceded him (that is, until he was tried as a heretic and had his tongue cut out and his right hand cut off). He was posthumously recognized as a saint. In a letter to his friend Thallasius, he asked, "If God already finished creating the world in six days, what is he doing now?"[16] Some have tried to answer this question by positing a kind of watchmaker role to the divinity. The divine creates, and sits back and watches the mechanics roll along and do their job. In other words, God is still resting on the seventh day.

Others see God's role in the universe like a builder/contractor. He built it and appears once in a while to fix it when it goes horribly wrong. Still others see God's warm presence in the cosmos, helping things along the way by sending books, divine messengers, special signs and generally cheering us on. In some ancient religions, there are many divinities. These may be able to bend the universe to fit their needs but are really just as constrained to it as we are, except they are bigger, more powerful and usually quite fickle if we get a sacrifice or a word of prayer wrong.

For Maximus, however, the cosmos expresses

the living heart of its creator. But just as Ella and the rabbinic scholar observed, the cosmos is still being created and still growing into further perfection. "God," Maximus wrote, "completed the primary principles [the Greek word here is *logoi*, the plural of *logos*] of creatures, and the universal essences of beings, once for all." In other words, the essence of what makes a star a star, a human a human and a dolphin a dolphin were brought into being at the beginning. "Yet, He is still at work, not only preserving these creatures in their very existence," that is, providing for them, "but effecting the formation, progress, and sustenance of the individual parts that are potential within them."[17] Each essence created is carefully developed into a multitude of particulars. So God took the essence of a human being, the principles that make a human being unique from the dolphin or the star, and He started producing actual human beings, like you and me and William Shakespeare.

But there is more. "Even now, in His providence, He is bringing about the assimilation of particulars to universals ... through the movement of these particular creatures toward well-being, and mak[ing] them harmonious and self-moving, in relation to one another, and to the whole universe." In his dense, philosophical way, Maximus is saying that each thing that comes into existence is being fashioned to fit into the whole cosmic picture. God is a poet, using grammar and poetics to fashion lines of poetry, and though each line is unique, it also fits into the larger poem, which would be incomplete without it. "Everything," he declares, "shall be unique, but everything shall express each other thing. Everything shall be in perfect harmony to one another ... one and the same principle shall be observable throughout the universe, though there may be many principles and many unique expressions of it."[18] Each unique thing will express the universal order, and the universal order will be revealed in each unique thing! "To see a World in a Grain of Sand," as William Blake put it, "And a Heaven in a Wild Flower, / Hold Infinity in the palm of your hand / And Eternity in an hour."[19]

The Dearest Freshness Deep Down Things

A question comes up at this point that is of great significance to ecology and natural philosophy. Is a thing sacred in itself? Many theistic traditions, including some forms of Christianity, believe that a thing only expresses the creator and has no intrinsic value or substance beyond this. Some religions would take the very different position that a thing is indeed sacred in itself, expressing nothing beyond this. The truth, I believe, holds both positions in harmony while introducing a further dimension.

The 19th-century poet-priest Gerard Manley Hopkins was one of many naturalists of his time who were concerned with the rising tide of industrial capitalism. He watched his English and Welsh countryside quickly transform at the hands of "dark Satanic Mills" (to borrow Blake's vivid phrase)[20] and the gradual exploitation of the earth for minerals, especially coal. Hopkins is a "minor poet" in the English literary canon, due mainly to the paucity of his overall corpus. However, his poetry and journals offer a major contribution to ecological philosophy and naturalism. I believe he is one of the finest, most comprehensive spiritual ecologists in English, even if he is challenging to understand.

His poem "God's Grandeur" deserves to be quoted here and discussed in full. I encourage

everyone to memorize it and read it out loud outdoors over and over again, especially if children are
around:

> The world is charged with the grandeur of God.
>> It will flame out, like shining from shook foil;
>> It gathers to a greatness, like the ooze of oil
> Crushed. Why do men then now not reck his
>>> rod?
> Generations have trod, have trod, have trod;
>> And all is seared with trade; bleared, smeared
>>> with toil;
>> And wears man's smudge and shares man's
>>> smell: the soil
> Is bare now, nor can foot feel, being shod.
> And for all this, nature is never spent;
>> There lives the dearest freshness deep down
>>> things;
> And though the last lights off the black West
>> went
>> Oh, morning, at the brown brink eastward,
>>> springs –
> Because the Holy Ghost over the bent
>> World broods with warm breast and with ah!
>>> bright wings.[21]

Hopkins unpacks that first line, "The world is charged with the grandeur of God," in a letter to Robert Bridges, Poet Laureate of England at the time and one of his closest friends: "All things therefore are charged with love, are charged with God and if we know how to touch them give off sparks, and take fire, yield drops and flow rings and tell of him."[22] So the world is charged – electrified, vivified – and reveals the grandeur and the presence of God as we touch and experience it. Hopkins then expresses this revealed presence in another image, that of "the ooze of oil crushed." He is referring to the Biblical symbol of the olive, which, when crushed, oozes out the king-making, athlete-anointing, light-bringing oil. The world is alive for Hopkins and, when pressed, expresses life and beauty.

Hopkins then asks an important question: "Why do men then now not reck his rod?" He envisions the sacred radiance revealed in the natural world as the "rod" of the creator, the shepherd's staff that leads and protects us. Personally, I feel this shows just how original a thinker he was. Hopkins, like John Muir, points us to the natural world as the locus for revelation and daily guidance, and in doing so roots us in spiritual ecology. So why, then, do we not "reck his rod"? In other words, why don't we listen to what all this glory reveals to us? "Generations have trod, have trod, have trod" upon this world, and "all is seared with trade," meaning we have commodified everything for trading, searing it as if with a brand, and in doing so missing the glory of it that is as brilliant as "shook foil."

I'm reminded of when Antoine de Saint-Exupéry's Little Prince comes to the planet of the businessman and asks him, "What are you doing?" The businessman says, "I'm counting the stars." "Why are you counting the stars?" asks the Little Prince. "Because I own the stars. If I count the stars then I own the stars." "How can you own the stars?" the Prince rejoins. "If I count them," replies the businessman, "I make them mine, I own them." Perplexed, the Little Prince asks, "What good can you do with the stars if you own them? They're no good to you." "That doesn't matter," grumps the businessman, "I own them."[23] And so trade takes that which is God's creation and commodifies it, creating a kind of slavery as a result.

Hopkins also points out that "the soil is bare

now, nor can foot feel, being shod." The soil itself has been tortured, overused, exploited. We have subjected the material that provides us with our food to strip mines, coal mines, fracking, degenerative farming, clear-cut logging, factory contamination and much more. We do not notice the effects of "trade" on the soil directly because we are "shod." Hopkins is referring to a detail in the book of Exodus where Moses, standing in front of the burning bush, is instructed by God to "take off your shoes, for where you stand is holy ground" (Exod. 3:5). Moses is being told he must commune with the sacred in an unmediated way. He must connect directly with the earth, sole to soil. When we look at our own society, we are almost always living such a mediated experience. We rarely have bare feet, and rarely connect directly to the natural world. The streets, suburbs, houses and technologies, indeed just about everything we see, are mediated through human design and through human eyes. This may be why our culture does not really have a place anymore for sacred ground, and even less genuine connection with anything of this grandeur of God.

Yet Hopkins makes an important claim in the

final six lines of the sonnet. "And, for all this," he announces, "nature is never spent." No matter how distant and fragmented our experience of the environment becomes, no matter how much we exploit and abuse it, we cannot stop nature from being a sacrament of the divine. Why? Because "there lives the dearest freshness deep down things." "Deep" and "down," with their descending phonetic *ee* and *ow* placed next to each other have the effect of bringing us right into the depth of things where the poet wants us to discover this indestructible "dearest freshness." I have been calling for a widespread elevation of awareness of nature all my adult life, and have often felt abject discouragement at what seems to be a losing battle. I know this is the experience of everyone working for the environment, whether through policy, adaptation or preservation. This poem offers a clarion call for all of us.

In one of the most original moments in 19th-century verse, Hopkins then reveals this "dearest freshness." Pointing to the western horizon, the region of darkness, the poet writes: "And though the last lights off the black West went," describing the last moments of the starless night. Then, turning to the east, the region of light, he says: "Oh, morning, at the brown brink eastward, springs." Springs! He's connecting through rhyme that which is "deep down things" with the "morning" eastwardly springing, and he does so with a word order that makes this morning lift off from its perch on the eastern firmament. He is describing a new creation that is constantly springing into the world. The first moments of the universe are springing through everything. This is Dylan Thomas's "The force that through the green fuse drives the flower,"[24] and it cannot be stopped or hindered.

Being a Christian, Hopkins describes the morning this way: "Because the Holy Ghost over the bent / World broods with warm breast and with ah! bright wings." He imagines the freshness deep down things like a mothering bird, imparting life-giving warmth into the world and spreading throughout the universe like bright wings. Hopkins is referencing the great poetry of the first chapter of Genesis, in which the image of the Holy Spirit moves over the face of the deeps and brings forth light from the turbulent waters. Basil the Great, a fourth-century theologian from Cappadocia, describes the Holy Spirit in Genesis as brooding over the face of the formless deep "as

we believe, and that our natural world is every-where a revelation of this language.

The End of Theology

"If you are a theologian, you will pray truly. And if you pray truly, you are a theologian."[26] This is a dictum I love from Evagrius of Pontus, an in-fluential and controversial monastic theologian of the fourth century. "Theology" is a compound Greek word derived from *theos* and *logos*, mean-ing "words/discussions concerning God." Left at its definition, theology appears to be an abstract, academic pursuit with little practical application. I love Evagrius's little dictum because it elevates the-ology to its true perch in the human heart. When we express gratitude to a divinity, or offer praise, or ask for help, or ask questions of the universe, we are using theology. Certainly we write books and say many things about God, but when ad-dressing the divine directly, we put those words into action. Theology is an affirmation of what we know about God and the world created. A living theology, one might say a purpose-fulfilled theol-ogy, is one that applies those affirmations to the divine directly. Thus, theology is the *content* of our prayer life. Evagrius makes the further point that we must pray truly, meaning that we must be sure that what we are saying is borne out by experience, tested through the ages and universally considered true. What we say *about* God has a major impact on what we say *to* God.

Not all affirmations, however, are theology. We can all make affirmational statements about our experience with the divine, but a theological affirmation is a very different thing. When we speak from within our tradition concerning God, we speak theologically, and in so speaking we are also in dialogue and being informed by the tradition itself. I have always been thrilled by this dynamic exchange between our affirmations of God and the tradition from which they arise. I only experience the dynamism, however, when this exchange is in response to the presence of the divine. This is why I can't see any truer statement than that of Evagrius about theology reaching its purpose when it becomes our prayer.

I have been told on a number of occasions that theology is a subject that only really matters to the religious, but I believe that we ignore the faith traditions of our world at our peril. The fact is that theologies of various sorts have been the midwives to many a nation throughout history, and their influence can be found in many aspects of modern Western life. What we say to and about God determines what we say to and about the world. This, in my opinion, is one of the reasons we are experiencing such a serious ecological crisis today. The theologies that shaped the Industrial Revolution and the constitutions of our countries have a clear and present impact on our current environmental policies.

For example, in 2006 several dozen prominent evangelical Protestant Christians in the United States signed a document (the Evangelical Climate Initiative) stating their acknowledgement of the realities and dangers of climate change and urging Christian responsibility to care for the planet. In the broader narrative of the environmental debate, this was hardly a controversial statement. However, despite early gains, this movement was not widely accepted within evangelical Protestantism at the time and was pretty much dead by 2009.[27] The environmental theology adopted by these evangelical Protestants dates back to the emerging Industrial Revolution in 19th-century Protestant

England. As we entered the world of coal mines, factories and the mass production of goods, various verses from the Bible took on new popular meaning. One such verse comes from Genesis: "And God said to them, 'Be fruitful and multiply, and fill the earth, and subdue it; and rule over the fish of the sea and over the birds of the sky and over every living thing that moves on the earth'" (Gen. 1:28). The words "subdue" and "rule" were held up to the congregations of the emerging modern world as evidence that God was telling us to mine the mountains, troll the seas, scathe the mountainsides for timber, and in so doing, usher in a prosperity that was our destiny to enjoy. And who could have known otherwise to disagree? Our resources seemed as limitless as our ingenuity in using them. No one could have imagined then that we were setting down a path to irreversible environmental change. That Genesis verse took on a significant role and was soon quoted more than it had ever been in the past.

Other verses with other sentiments, such as Genesis 2:15 or 3:23, which describe our role on earth as servants and tillers of the land, were backgrounded to the subduing theology of Genesis 1 that suited the zeitgeist. There is really no way to soften the fact that when Genesis uses the word "subdue" in both Hebrew and Greek, it literally means to place your foot on the neck of your conquered enemy, signifying a submission of the enemy to his defeater.

These Biblical verses were not interpreted so literally and with such passion before the Industrial Revolution. The subjugation of the earth means something quite different when you encounter a raw, wild, barren, hostile terrain, such as the early peoples of Mesopotamia did (from which we derive the book of Genesis). Genesis 1:28 is describing (and encouraging) our efforts to carve out a place in the robust and wild earth. Reading accounts of the early settlers in North America, one understands just how important it was to subdue the earth – digging out tree roots, defending our homesteads from wolves, redirecting water for drinking and irrigation, finding food in an intractable landscape and so on. However, this kind of subduing was of a very different character than that promoted in the pulpits of a 19th-century Protestantism giddy with the advances and seemingly limitless prosperity of the modern age.

In a curious irony, just as church and state were separating in the United States and the rest of the modern world, a new collusion was formed between the pulpit and the business world. As the American industrial complex grew, so too did the belief that our subduing of the earth for economic reasons was the stated plan of God all along (i.e., to be fruitful and multiply). Other verses were highlighted, taken out of context, held up as examples and used to justify the formation of a new American way of life. This is why the environmental movement failed, at least at first, to take root in some Protestant evangelical churches, and why it failed especially at a time when the economy, largely due to the subprime mortgage crisis of 2006, was teetering and seemed ready to collapse.

The religious movements that shaped the formation of the country itself and justified the industrial complex that built it face a direct challenge in the face of climate change and economic reform. Those who were foolish enough to propose that creation care[28] is a theology that is consistent with Christian theology in general were not wrong in doing so; they were just ahead of their time. In fact, a creation-care theology is consistent when God is speaking to us. How can we discern God's voice from our own? This an important question, because in asking it we are avoiding the temptation to confuse our own voice with God's. I can only really answer this question from my own experience and that of the spiritual masters over the ages.

In my life, God has spoken to me in two distinct ways. The first has been a direct revelation of divine presence. In these cases, I heard the voice of God radiate throughout my being as if it was coming from a place deeper within me than my own consciousness. I felt as though I was caught up in an eternal moment while the rest of life swirled around me like a river around a rock. The voice was not exactly audible, but it was unmistakably that of my creator; it was absolutely authoritative and I recognized it at once as the voice that called my being into being. I also recognized that this presence was a loving one. In fact, it was a love that had a divine, uncreated origin. In this presence I knew two things: that I was loved, and that I was created in and for and through this love. I also knew that I was utterly unworthy of this love.

"Unworthy" is a strong word, but I can't change

what I felt. It was as if God's love was too immense to challenge; it held me in its divine arms, and always would, but I knew I would never be able to match or understand or stop it. I felt at first like a grumpy kid suddenly hugged and squirming in the discomfort of it. I wanted only to fall down before it, and on two occasions did so. There was nothing left for me except silence and the final acceptance of a love beyond my ken.

In this love, I understood that the already created me, and no other self-creation, is the ground of the divine encounter, where God knows me and I discover God. I have had this experience of God four times in my life – when I was a teen and was ushered into a quest for the divine; when I became a Christian and learned (without knowing how or why) that I must also be a priest; when I was baptized into the Eastern Orthodox Church; and shortly after I became a single father with a new vocation: to raise three girls.

The second way in which I have known the voice of God is through the beauty of the natural world. I have been transformed by it in several ways. I realized that I was part of something that was much greater than myself – a system of created orders that included and also passed infinitely beyond me. Understanding this lifted me out of my state of isolation and put me in direct relationship to the whole of the cosmos. "When we try to pick out anything by itself," said John Muir, "we find it hitched to everything else in the Universe."[29] Further, I learned that I was part of that beauty. I not only stood as a witness to the beauty of the cosmos but also was just as beautiful as it and everything in it. I was a voice of God too, transmitting to the universe His presence and love. I have stood on promontories in the mountains, knelt before flowers aglow in the sun, watched an eagle swoop and sweep above me, heard the call of loons over a dark blue lake veiled in white morning mist and I have been refreshed in my soul by the living beauty I experienced. Here again, John Muir speaks to the truth: "Everybody needs beauty as well as bread, places to play in and pray in, where nature may heal and give strength to body and soul alike."[30]

Some years ago, I climbed a mountain in Wells Gray Provincial Park, BC, while on a week-long wilderness trek with 12 others. We would hold seminars in the morning around the campfire and hike in the afternoon. On this occasion, we were camped at a remote glacial lake and decided to canoe to the base of a mountain nearby, then bushwhack our way to the peak. It was an arduous and dangerous exercise, but once at the top we were afforded 360-degree views of the mountains, lakes and glaciers. The scene was too immense to take in. We sat on the peak in silent awe. Our words were just too paltry for what was around us. I pulled out my pocket Bible and started reading the final chapters of the book of Job.

The book of Job is about the fate of a man with great wealth and deep devotion to God. Satan, a name in Hebrew that means "accuser," approaches God and challenges him to test the faith of Job by letting him take away all of Job's wealth and happiness. God permits him to do this, and within a chapter Satan destroys Job's estate and kills his family, except his wife, who tells Job only to "curse God and die" (Job 2:9). Job, however, remains faithful while sitting on a heap of ashes and demanding an answer for why he is suffering. (I always thought Job's greatest affliction came in the form of his three friends, who each in their turn explain to Job that he is responsible for his the message from those words was twofold. This world, with its complex ecosystems and immeasurable variety, is beyond our ability to understand or control. We belong to it, but we do not own it. But, just as importantly, this creation is beautiful and its beauty conveys God's presence – and even His answer – to our suffering. Job's answer is splendid: "I have heard of Thee by the hearing of the ear; But now my eye sees Thee; Therefore I retract, and I repent in dust and ashes" (Job 42:5–6). He at first knew and believed in God based solely on what he had *heard* about Him, but now, having seen God revealed in the beauty of his creation, he is soothed and humbled. When I read these verses on that summit, the words became the mountains and the mountains became the words and both expressed the beauty of God in the natural world.

The human experience of beauty brings us directly into the presence of the divine in several ways. First, we encounter transcendence. Much of our daily life is consumed with getting, spending, building, selling, eating and interacting with people and surroundings in materialistic or carnal ways. There is little sense of what is beyond what we see and do. Beauty pulls back the veil from this basic way of life and reveals something more. We are not taken out of this world by beauty; that is, we do not transcend our world. On the contrary, we enter into a richer relationship with it. In the presence of beauty, we see our world as a gift, radiating an otherness and a "thisness" both at once; it is as though we recognize heaven as being earthly and earth as being heavenly. We transcend our material existence by seeing a glimpse of the spiritual realities everywhere within it.

In this moment of transcendence, we encounter the *character* of beauty, which is holiness. Beauty is holy. I believe this is the reason I feel unworthy whenever I am in its presence; I am at that moment aware of how unaware I am, most of the time, of the holiness of life. It's as if someone walked out from a crowd and said, "Here I am, your beautiful friend!" My sadly inadequate response being, "I barely know you, and yet you are everywhere with me!" Beauty reveals a holiness that is a wild otherness, an uncontainable, unapproachable, incomprehensible life in life. I gaze through beauty at God and I am humbled like Job. What is so remarkable to me is that this holiness is radically present in this world. Isaac Newton marvelled at catch sight of the bursting, pink-white glory of a flowering cherry tree, and in that beauty, however long it lasts in chronological time, I have nowhere else to be; indeed, everywhere and everything else is gathered with me into the stillness of that encounter. What's more, I am gathered too. When "The world is too much with us," to borrow from William Wordsworth, and "Getting and spending, we lay waste our powers,"[31] the human being becomes fragmented. Worries and tasks carry us in many directions at once. The encounter with beauty pulls all these strands together, focuses them into one whole person and holds us in an eternal now. In such a moment, God has pitched His tent in our hearing.

There is also a sadness, however, that I feel in the face of beauty. Years ago, my then 5-year-old daughter Ella rushed into the house and told me to come outside. I followed her of course, and when outside she told me to look up at the stars, which were thick and bright. I remember a strong wind that played in the leaves of the trees. She put her hand in mine and squeezed it tightly. She said, "Dad, we can fly up there and be in the stars together. Keep holding my hand. Let's go!" I felt her body lift into her imagination. Her hand tightened in mine. I looked up too, and felt the beauty of this moment keenly. I also felt extremely sad. I knew she would return to the house soon enough, and that this moment would leave with her. How could I hold on to it? I felt a sort of cruelty then, as if it were unfair that I should have such an experience and never have it again. Sure, I could always remember it, and I have, but this was a poor consolation then, as it is now.

Ever since, I have taken note of this sadness in my experience of the beautiful. It feels like a human predicament, stuck, it seems, in a temporal, chronological existence. The sadness feels like an imposition of self-awareness that breaks the spell of transcendence. Try as I do, I cannot avoid it. There is no denying the transcendence, holiness, presence and stillness of beauty, but there is no avoiding the departure, the fragility, the transience of its manifestation. I have wondered whether all the moments of beauty I have been blessed to experience will be recollected, even recapitulated, at some point in my dying or after my death. But this always feels like an empty hope, somehow off the mark. I suppose we could say that beauty's fleeting nature should inspire us to live in hope and patience for some future heaven to do away with time. But time is beautiful too. Time is a creation as much as anything else. Our temporal existence is not a problem that a heaven needs to solve. In my faith tradition, heaven is not a place somewhere else; it is everywhere present and filling all things, revealing itself, as I have said, in the presence of beauty.

But I now accept, and embrace, this sadness because I see such moments as lessons. We learn through beauty what the world we live in really is and we trace over a lifetime the face of God in this revelation. I therefore see the experience of beauty as an ascetic exercise in which I actively apply the revelation to the rest of my life. The sadness I feel inspires a discipline of seeing that results in my seeing always and everywhere what is revealed to me in those moments.

But there is another reason why I believe that beauty must somehow be veiled by time. In many spiritual traditions around the world a veil is used to cover what is holy. In Western cultures today, however, a veil is quite the opposite. If we are proud of something, we show it off, we reveal it.

Otherwise, we are hiding something and therefore must feel ashamed of it in some way. This is most prevalent in how we dress. I once shared with a group of people my belief that modesty in dress is an expression of self-love. I was immediately criticized for shaming women! My intention was quite the opposite. I believe men and women who dress with modesty are saying that their bodies are sacred and beautiful and should not be flaunted for everyone to lust after. They are kept veiled in mystery for the person who takes the time to see the worth in a person. Modesty is a veil to cover the sacred, which will only be revealed to the one who will honour it as such. I am using modesty here as a synonym for mystery – because the modesty of the creator produces the mysteries of the universe, material or otherwise. This beautiful, sacred-bearing cosmos is veiled from us until we either see it as a gift or seek it as we would seek the face of our beloved.

Beauty Will Save the World

I want to turn now to the words I used for the title of this chapter, "Beauty Will Save the World." The quote comes from Dostoevsky's *The Idiot*, where it is a simple phrase that is given no explanation. At a dinner party, a character named Hippolyte makes a speech in which he asks the protagonist, Prince Myshkin, if it is true "that you once declared that 'beauty would save the world'? Great Heaven! The prince says that beauty saves the world!"[32] Hippolyte goes on to say that the only reason the prince might have said such a thing is that he is in love. The prince does not respond at all, and we never know what he really said. We do know, however, that he has fallen in love. The novel ends rather calamitously, and given the extent of the characters' suffering, we are justified in thinking that whether or not the prince did say it, beauty certainly didn't save anyone in his world.

The phrase itself, however, has a way of getting into one's head and then, over a lifetime, working its way into one's heart. Aleksandr Solzhenitsyn, when he was awarded the Nobel Prize for literature in 1970, discussed this quote in his acceptance speech. "One day," said Solzhenitsyn, "Dostoyevsky threw out the enigmatic remark: 'Beauty will save the world.' What sort of a statement is that? For a long time I considered it mere words. How could that be possible? When in marriage, the loss of a career, a house, a car, a library and many other priceless things. There was upheaval everywhere and it took all my strength just to hold on to my three daughters while trying to give them as many good memories as I could so they would know they were loved before, during and after everything. It all felt like too much. I questioned everything, railed at God and generally crashed about, hoping for an end someday to the pain and confusion. Reading Solzhenitsyn's speech helped me see that suffering is a part of life and that an honest life will have a fair share of it. Suffering is as common to life as eating, and being shocked by it, hiding from it, treating it like it is unnatural, is just to make it worse. So I turned toward it, and faced myself in doing so.

Shortly after reading Solzhenitsyn, I read Viktor Frankl's *Man's Search for Meaning*, and discovered there just such an example of how beauty pierces our sorrows. Frankl, like Solzhenitsyn, was a survivor of a concentration camp, specifically Dachau. After the war, he developed a type of therapy called logotherapy, based directly on his experiences in Dachau and his observations of the psychic and spiritual effects of suffering

through the enveloping gloom. I felt it transcend that hopeless, meaningless world, and
from somewhere I heard a victorious "Yes" in
answer to my question of the existence of an
ultimate purpose. At that moment a light was
lit in a distant farmhouse, which stood on
the horizon as if painted there, in the midst
of the miserable grey of a dawning morning in Bavaria. "*Et lux in tenebris lucet*" – and
the light shineth in the darkness ... Then, at
that very moment, a bird flew down silently
and perched just in front of me, on the heap
of soil which I had dug up from the ditch, and
looked steadily at me.[34]

In these moments, Frankl hears God's voice
rise up from within him and become manifest
in the living, affirmational presence of beauty.
Frankl was Jewish, but what he described is everywhere, in all manner of spiritual literature. I
know it as my experience too. I remember standing at the edge of a Hawaiian beach, admittedly
in vastly happier circumstances, watching in awe
as a massive storm surge scraped back tons of sand,
revealing the solid black lava bed beneath. In that

moment, a voice rose up from within me saying, "Rebuild upon Me." I knew what it meant and it was life-affirming. Beauty is the power of God's voice transforming suffering.

A form of Japanese pottery sums this up well. In the 16th century, it is said, the shogun Ashikaga Yoshimasa sent a precious, damaged, Chinese tea bowl back to China. There it was repaired in a crude fashion, which prompted a Japanese crafts-man to find a new and more aesthetically pleas-ing way to fix it. What emerged was *kintsugi*, a method of repairing broken pottery using gold or other precious metals for joinery. The philosophy behind *kintsugi* is that the piece is more beautiful for having been broken. In an essay on the subject, Christy Bartlett offers these observations concern-ing the aesthetic principles of the method:

> [The repaired pottery] becomes an eternally present moment yet a moment that oddly enough segues into another where perishabil-ity is circumvented by repair. Simultaneously we have the expression of frailty and of re-silience, life before the incident and life after. Yet the object is not the same. In its rebirth it

assumes a new identity that incorporates yet transcends the previous identity.[35]

Thus, the gold veins holding the broken shards together express the fact that our brokenness and suffering are not the end of life but a new beginning, a beginning in which the healing itself is revealed as the beauty at the heart of life. As Leonard Cohen sings in "Anthem": "There is a crack, a crack in everything / That's how the light gets in."[36]

So beauty is the language of God in life, in the presence of which all our theological affirmations about the divine must fall silent – not because they are worthless but because they are just our side of the conversation. The entire conversation takes place in a world that is always being created and through which the creator is always expressing itself. But what of us? What is our place in all this grandeur of God and the beauty transforming us through it? In order to answer these questions, and soon to arrive at our altars, we need to venture further and explore the wildernesses that are our own.

CHAPTER THREE
The Wilderness Temple

Our Temple

There are two kinds of temples: those we build and those God builds. Ours are made of stone, wood, clay, gold and glass. God's are made of mountains, forests, earth, rivers, sand, water and the human heart. I am not interested in which one is superior. My grandmother used to say that comparisons are odious, and I try to avoid them wherever possible. I am concerned, however, with the importance of a clear understanding of the origins and purposes of each. The temples we make can represent the heights of the human spirit. The temple of Solomon, for instance, was legendary in the ancient world for its unmatched splendour and exhibition of faith in gold, cedar and precious jewels. The temple of Hagia Sophia (Holy Wisdom), built by the emperor Justinian in the sixth century in

Constantinople, was not only the greatest feat of engineering in its time (it still stands today, having endured countless earthquakes and the ravages of history) but was also adorned with the finest mosaics and metalwork known to the world. According to legend, when the structure was completed and the emperor was approaching it for the first time in the opening procession, he remarked, "Solomon, I have outdone thee!" Hagia Sophia ranks among the great temples of India, Japan, Tibet, ancient Greece and Rome, medieval Europe and the Mayan Yucatán, all of them gloriously revealing in their structures the genius of their respective cultures and our ingenuity as a species.

Human hands have been building temples in settlements, villages and cities ever since we moved from a nomadic existence to an agrarian one. The act is not only as ancient as human society itself but spans all cultures and places. Only a few hundred years ago we gave our species a name, *Homo sapiens*, meaning humans of wisdom. This makes sense because one thing that separates us from other species is our ability to learn and apply knowledge. However, Father Alexander Schmemann, an Eastern Orthodox priest and luminary of in these places. Some churches I have visited have been built to resemble auditoriums and even double as gymnasiums, complete with markings for basketball and floor hockey. I have been in Hindu temples and Muslim mosques that resemble hotel conference halls more than they do their often magnificent prototypes in India or the Middle East. On the one hand, this is totally understandable; we live in an age that has given us cheap, mass-produced components and it is a rare congregation that has the capital to spend on specialized tradespeople and expensive natural materials these days. A simple arch, for instance, is now an architectural luxury. I have sat on building committees myself, even chaired them as a priest, and I know how hard it is to think beyond the "get it built as cheaply and fast as you can" mentality. But I also believe that in adopting this type of thinking we have abandoned our origins as faith communities, and in doing so, we end up with temples that reflect mere utility and not the beauty they are meant to inspire and reflect.

Early in the 20th century, the Russian Orthodox Church convened an extraordinary meeting of hierarchs and church leaders, the first of its kind in centuries, to discuss matters of worship, organization and church governance. The results would have brought historic changes to a church that badly needed reform had it not been for the revolution that broke out soon after. However, it is worth noting that the topic of electric lighting in the temple was addressed in one of the synodal meetings. The light bulb was still a fresh innovation and no one can blame the churches for rushing to introduce it. However, the consensus at the meeting was that the light bulb should only be used advisedly in worship, since the quality of light it produced was essentially different from that of a candle or oil lamp.

I agree. I have been in temples for evening services where the lights are full on and found it a jarring experience compared to those where the only illumination was from dozens of little flames. But for me the most important observation in this Russian document was the fact that turning on a light in the temple was a utilitarian act compared to the lighting of a candle, which was an offertory one. More than this, the candles themselves are usually made of beeswax, which gives off a pleasing aroma and is completely natural. I still love the fact that after lighting a candle in the church, my hands smell of wax; I delight in the tactility of it. Temple lamps burn olive oil, which has been used for millennia to light homes, palaces and places of worship. I visited one church in Monemvasia, Greece, at the southern tip of the Peloponnese, which had a centuries-old olive tree growing beside it for the sole purpose of harvesting olives to make oil for the lamps.

In my own church, we made a heroic effort to return to natural building materials and resources in worship. I was the priest of All Saints of Alaska Orthodox Church in Victoria, BC, which I founded, from 2002 until 2011. I felt incredibly blessed by the opportunity to serve such a vibrant, forward-thinking community. In 2006 we adopted a 100-mile diet for all things pertaining to public worship. We sourced locally produced beeswax for our candles, used local wood for our furniture, made our own wine, started growing and grinding wheat for church bread, harvested tree sap for incense and even sourced some olive trees growing on one of the Gulf Islands for our lamps. Electric light was used only minimally and never at full brightness. We stopped using disposable needs of the poor before the needs of the temple. Why fill our temples with art and gold while ignoring the hungry, the thirsty and the destitute? I have sympathy with this line of thinking to a point. I felt so strongly in the axiom that food for me is an economic problem but food for my neighbour is a moral one that I worked to the point of exhaustion, establishing an outreach centre for poor and low-income families in Victoria as part of my ministry. However, as pragmatic as such arguments appear to be, they ignore one very important fact. The temple itself can be an offering of beauty to the poor and destitute in this world. I have been poor, at least as poor as you can be in a First World society. I have been homeless and visited food lines and food banks just to survive. What's more, I did it while trying to care for my three girls. But I never felt robbed of food or overlooked when I encountered beauty in the temples of worship I visited. Beauty ennobles a human being; it elevates our spirits and offers hope and transcendence. A family suffering from poverty in daily life can feel rich with the beauty of their temple. Where else can we drink from gold chalices, see and touch expensive fabrics, enjoy the aroma of fine spices and hear the practised eloquence of calls to prayer and hymns written by the poets through the ages?

In one Christian gospel, the story is told of a woman, a harlot in fact, who pushes her way into a room where Jesus is sitting as a guest with the spiritual leaders of his day. She brought with her fine spices and ointments in extravagant quantities (enough to cost a year's wage) and poured it all on the feet of Jesus. She even took off her head covering and washed his feet with her hair. In the ancient world of Jesus's day, this was an extraordinary outpouring of affection and love. And of course, she was met with the same argument. Why could she not have sold the ointment and given the money to the poor? But love doesn't always abide by the line items of our budgets; it pours itself out where it will. Beauty is an offering to the poor as much as food is. When we pour beauty out at the feet of the poor, we love them as much as the woman loved her deliverer, Jesus.

There is another reason why we must seriously consider how we construct our temples and worship experience. We are bound to the laws, seasons and ecosystems of our natural world. Time is just one example. How we keep time now bears almost no resemblance to how we have kept it through history. The diminution of our days into hours, minutes and seconds was a big change from the keeping of time according to the location of the sun or moon in the sky. Though keeping time this way has its roots in the expansion of our world through nautical exploration, not to mention the adoption of clocks in European society, the real shift came with the advent of the Industrial Revolution and the need to organize and pay the workforce. More specifically, in an effort to increase profits by maximizing productivity, the workforce was subjugated to a system of exact timekeeping, which has dominated modern life ever since. While this presents a serious challenge for the organizationally impaired, like me, this way of timekeeping is not a moral problem. After all, it did help accomplish immense productivity and prosperity (chiefly for the occidental economies).

However, it does present a problem for historic faiths built on the natural cycles of the day, month and year. The Muslim calls to prayer and the daily liturgical cycles of certain churches, for instance, are based on solar, not clock, time. The third, sixth and ninth hours are concepts that are unknown today and yet still govern worship in many traditions. I wonder what is lost in organizing our days according to clocks rather than the rising and setting of the sun? Time disconnected from the natural world becomes numbers on a cell phone, alarm clock or car radio. The earliest recorded post-Biblical hymn of the Christian church, known for its first line, *phos hilaron*, "Gladsome Light," was sung by the faithful just as the sun was setting.[38] They would gather in their temple and light the lamps for the evening, taking care to light their own lamps to take home with them. In this way, the cycle of the day and the spiritual life were seamlessly intertwined.

The yearly cycle too was built into temple architecture and life. Planting and harvest seasons had their feast days, as did the solstices. One's entire natural world, with its daily and yearly cycles, was drawn into and given meaning by the temples at the heart of our communities.

We are always inspired by examples of early architecture that convey extraordinary, astronomical precision. For instance, the stairs of a Mayan temple in Chichén Itzá cast a shadow in the shape of a snake on one religiously significant day of the year.[39] Countless other examples exist. While these are genuine feats of astronomical knowledge, they nonetheless represent a common experience and connection with the natural world that modern timekeeping does not seem to inspire, despite the precision it offers.

I am not suggesting that we become spiritual Luddites in our approach to our temples, though I can't see it being a real problem if we did. I am also not against modern construction practices or even the use of synthetic materials. I think there is a place for such things when used advisedly and in moderation. What I am saying is that those of us who still build temples should take a serious look at what we are saying to the world and to ourselves when we build them without a single reference to nature. A predominantly synthetic and utilitarian temple architecture says we can have a faith and life that are independent of the natural world of our creator. Spiritual ecology is rendered a secondary interest to the faith tradition when we worship God outside of and without reference to His creation. A spiritual life is nothing when not a bodily one. Humans have five powerful senses through which we interact with the world and each other. Yet so many of our temples now might give us something to hear, sermons and hymns for instance, but there is little to look at, nothing to smell, touch or taste; these buildings inspire a worship that is an exercise in sensory deprivation.

I wish to give the final word on this subject to the celebrated Serbian poet and saint Nikolaj Velimirović. God does not need a temple, we do. We build them as reflections of our faith, which is why, if they are devoid of nature, they reflect a faith devoid of it as well. We build them to house worship of the creator and as expressions of the beauty we see everywhere around us. We build them as examples of what it means to be a human being fully alive. When we lose sight of this, our temples have no purpose. To this, Velimirović has some prophetic words:

> Can those who are themselves homeless really build the temple for the Teacher of all builders? ... When you build the best for Him, you are setting an example for your soul, showing her what she should be building within herself ... You build Him expensive edifices, in order to remind your soul that

she was intended for royal palace, and not
for hovels of clay … But what will become of
your temples … If the domes of your temples
are forever higher than your souls? … If the
width of your temples is forever wider than
the narrowness of your souls? … If your altars are forever shining more brightly than
all the shrines of your souls? … They will become the dead monuments of dead souls.[40]

The Wilderness Temple

On a summery day early in September 1875, John
Muir ventured out into his beloved Yosemite
wilderness. He did this often, of course, exploring and cataloguing the region he eventually
helped to establish as one of the earliest US na-
tional parks. For Muir, "going out" into the wilderness was really "going in"; he was more comfortable with the plants, animals and mountains
of the high Sierras than he was anywhere else.
Muir was a Scottish-born American pioneer of
wilderness exploration and is rightly considered
to be the father of modern ecology. Raised in a
strict Presbyterian family, he eventually became
a poet, a mystic, a fervent environmentalist and

a visionary. He would go to extremes to experience the power and beauty of nature, even on one occasion climbing a tree in a ferocious storm. "I am hopelessly and forever a mountaineer," he once said, "I care only to entice people to look at Nature's loveliness." Muir saw this loveliness everywhere he looked in his wilderness playground and he marvelled at the power of it: "How wonderful the power of beauty! Gazing awe-stricken, I might've left everything for it. Beauty beyond thought everywhere, beneath, above, made and being made forever."[41]

Muir believed that nature was a window to the divine, the source of God's first revelations, and he called everyone to find refreshment in them. "Oh, these vast, calm, measureless mountain days, inciting at once to work and rest! Days in whose light everything seems equally divine, opening a thousand windows to show us God. Nevermore, however weary, should one faint by the way who gains the blessings of one mountain day; whatever his fate, long life, short life, stormy or calm, he is rich forever."[42] His destination on that early September day was Cathedral Peak and he recorded in his journal his thoughts during the hike:

How often I have gazed at it [Cathedral Peak] from the tops of hills and ridges, and through openings in the forests on many short excursions, devoutly wondering, admiring, longing! This I may say is the first time I have been at church in California, led here at last, every door graciously opened for the poor lonely worshipper. In our best times everything turns into religion, all the world seems a church and the mountains altars. And lo, here at last in front of the Cathedral [Peak] is blessed cassiope [mountain heather] ringing her thousands of sweet-toned bells, the sweetest church music I ever enjoyed. Listening, admiring, until late in the afternoon I compelled myself to hasten away...[43]

I have carried this passage close to me for many years, never more so than in my most turbulent and difficult hours. Time and again, I would lace up my boots and head out for a hike, and find again in nature communion with God. I healed most in the mountains and, just as Muir describes, they became my altars and churches. I got used to seeing the stars again. I woke with the sun and grew tired and slept when it set. I started hearing birds for the first time in a long time, even discerning the varieties of their songs, especially in the morning. The longer I stayed out, the less I snacked; I ate heartily but only when I was hungry. My eyes stretched with the scenery, my chest opened and my heart grew full.

These things had a profound physiological effect on me. Our bodies carry our traumas and stress in our very tissues, sometimes for years. We are, in our own right, highly interconnected ecosystems. So the effects on me in these wilderness temples are always profound. I knew I was healing out there; I felt like I could come back to my faith community, ready and renewed to start again. The funny thing about healing is that in many ways we have no control over the process; it is something that happens to us when we allow it. Our opinion as to how it should happen is often irrelevant because healing proceeds in its own way and on its own time. But I am convinced of the truth of Muir's words about the wilderness temple and that all of us who wander into the wonder of it will commune with the divine and find some comfort there. In my case, the call back to the elemental temples of God came in the form of these words spoken by Jesus: "Come to Me, all who are weary and heavy-laden, and I will give you rest" (Matt. 11:28).

Wonder and play are two things we most associate with children. In the wilderness temple, we are all children and such things are serious business. Wonder opens us to the mysteries of what we behold. We follow it into the joy of our maker and there we play. I once built an altar on a mountainside and served at it with my companions. Surrounded as we were by so much natural beauty, the prayers we offered were carried by the winds into the meadows, forests, streams and mountains. When we were finished, we began jumping into icy pools, scrambling over riverbeds, sliding down rocks, laughing and shouting and exploring. We were at play in the fields of the Lord. I was reminded of the poetry of Dylan Thomas, who wrote best of all about the wonder we know as children. He often mourned its passing, in an echo of my own experience of sadness at beauty's passing: "Time held me green and dying / Though I sang in my chains like the sea." But in these great green temples of nature, we were free to chase each other "Down the rivers of the windfall light," and we felt as though "it was all / Shining, it was Adam and maiden," while around us "the sabbath rang slowly / In the pebbles of the holy streams."[44]

Being childlike is different from being childish. When Jesus commands his disciples to "permit the little children to come to me, for of such is the kingdom of God" (Luke 18:16), he is not only speaking literally of the children. This is also a command to become childlike, to recover a sense of belonging, of being parented by the divine. Here, in the chapels of nature, we are surrounded by every created thing, a living, flowering, buzzing cornucopia, and we realize that we are not isolated from the cosmos. Everything is being parented, and everything finds freedom to be just as it is in the same, grand, created household.

In one of the Apollo missions to outer space, a photo was taken that might be one of the most important humans have encountered: our earth, green and blue, surrounded by the infinite blackness of space. Some have said this picture changed the way we think about our world because for the first time we saw where we lived and how unique it is in the universe. We realized that we belong here and nowhere else, and that there is no "planet B." But a great many Christians hold the belief that this earth is a temporary residence, one that will be destroyed and replaced with a new one when God returns. Verses such as these from Peter's second letter are used to justify this belief: "But the day of the Lord will come like a thief, in which the heavens will pass away with a roar and the elements will be destroyed with intense heat, and the earth and its works will be burned up ... But according to His promise we are looking for new heavens and a new earth, in which righteousness dwells" (2 Pet. 3:10, 13). A similar sentiment is echoed in John's book of Revelation: "And I saw a new heaven and a new earth; for the first heaven and the first earth passed away, and there is no longer any sea." (Rev. 21:1)

The conundrum for those who read these verses literally is that no one for the first 18 centuries of Christian history interpreted them this way. In fact, the classical Christian teaching is quite the opposite: the earth we know today will be the earth God restores on the Last Day. Peter and John are using apocalyptic language to express the radical newness of what God will bring to the heavens and the earth. We are not facing a brand new earth but a renewed and transfigured one. Indeed, the earth will be transfigured to reveal everywhere in everything the shining presence of God in its midst. When John says, "God so loved the world, that He sent His only begotten son," the word he uses for world is "cosmos," meaning the whole of creation. In this way, according to classical Christian tradition, the whole cosmos is saved by the advent of God into it.

There is therefore no justification, save greed and ignorance, for treating this world as a temporary, and therefore exploitable, resource. Instead, if we are to read Revelation correctly, we might want to heed this statement: "... and Your wrath came, and the time came ... to destroy those who destroy the earth" (Rev. 11:18). Our own temples might be temporary, but those of God remain forever, which is another reason why I feel we must build the foundations of the former on the ground of the latter.

Instead, what would actually be burned away by the fire invoked in Revelation is not the planet Earth itself but what we have made of it. Some time back, I had a conversation with the abbot of a small monastery on British Columbia's Sunshine Coast. We were sitting at a table outdoors and I was pouring out my woes to him. We talked about the need to be just as we have been created and about how suffering can burn away the many false images we create for ourselves. I said I felt stripped and naked in a dark valley with nothing left to lose except my own life; these were dark times indeed. At this point, he placed his hand on the table and said, "I built this table. But do you think it will exist in the new earth?" I couldn't see why it wouldn't. "I'm not sure it will," he said. "The tree I built it from might exist there. The point is that nothing will be renewed that isn't made in the image of God. Even if you create a hundred false images of yourself, not one will endure."

Far from a place of loss and darkness, he saw my raw state as a gift of authenticity. This was the fresh perspective I needed. I was no longer trying to be someone or something else, and therefore, as an authentic creation, I could have a real relationship with my creator. Rather than looking past the earth we're on, to some new, 2.0 version of it, we must accept the earth as it is: our home, God's temple, an authentic creation, one that we must care for because it is a product of God and which he loved enough to save along with us and, perhaps at times, from us.

I recognize we have covered a lot of ground thus far. Indeed, we have travelled backward and forward in time, from the beginning to the end of things, and explored the languages of theology and God, and even ventured into our temple in the wilderness and the wilderness temple of God. It is now time to turn our attention to the altar we must build in the heart of it all and what purposes it fulfills.

CHAPTER FOUR
The Altar

There are two kinds of wilderness: the one we go into and the one we bring with us. Both are as dangerous as they are beautiful. Our wilderness, however, might be the wilder one. In third-century Alexandria, a young man named Anthony walked by a church during service. As he did so, he heard the following words read from the gospel of Saint Matthew: "If you would be perfect, go and sell that you have and give to the poor; and come follow Me and you shall have treasure in heaven" (19:21). According to the biography written by his friend Saint Athanasius, Anthony was struck to the heart. He sold his sizeable inheritance, gave the proceeds to his only sister and went out to the graves outside the city. In that culture, the bodies of the dead were placed in caves and this is where Anthony set about starting to pray. It was not long, however, before the devil took notice of this up-start Christian and attempted to ruin him with his first and usually most successful attack, that of lust. Anthony held fast, however, and so the devil, in his fury, sent demons to beat him until he was nearly dead. A friend came to visit Anthony with some nourishment and discovered him dying from bruiseless wounds on the cave floor. Taking him back to the church, he began to care for him.

Anthony waited until nightfall, then slipped out and, with the help of his friend, dragged himself back to the cave. In true Rocky Balboa style, he stood up and declared, "Here I am: Anthony." Incensed by this challenge, the devil sent the demons to charge at him as lions, bears, leopards, bulls, serpents, asps, scorpions, wolves and other terrifying beasts. Anthony stood his ground and even laughed, mocking the devil with these words: "If you were truly powerful, you would not need to appear as dumb beasts. Go ahead. Do your worst, if you can!" At this, the devil knew he was defeated by the courage and faith of Anthony and retreated to his darkness. The conqueror then ventured deeper into the desert wilderness and found a ruined citadel, and there he spent 20 years in spiritual combat with himself while a growing crowd of followers camped outside, waiting for him to finally emerge. When he did so, Anthony was transfigured, standing before them neither moved by their praise nor angered by their demands. He was triumphant, healthy and ready to teach and heal. "And they, when they saw him, wondered at the sight, for he had the same habit of body as before, and was neither fat, like a man without exercise, nor lean from fasting and striving with the demons, but he was just the same as they had known him before his retirement. And again his soul was free from blemish, for it was neither contracted as if by grief, nor relaxed by pleasure, nor possessed by laughter or dejection, for he was not troubled when he beheld the crowd, nor overjoyed at being saluted by so many."[45]

This is an iconic moment in Christian history, but it also represents a historic shift in how we began to view our environment. From the most ancient times, the wilderness outside our cities and villages was a terrifying place full of dangerous beasts and haunted people. These are our primal fears and they will always be with us, because we need them on some level to survive. What

Anthony did was, in Athanasius's words, make "the desert a city."[46] Soon, thousands of men and women poured out to the wilderness in order to follow Anthony, became hermits themselves or founded their own monastic communities. The wild, unknown places, once avoided at all costs, were directly challenged, even populated. But this outward movement was really an inward one. These people were seeing the desert as a place to find themselves; it was a journey to the heart, involving combat with forces more fearsome than wild animals. There had been hermits and desert communities before, of course – John the Baptist and the Essenes in the time of Jesus, for example – but nothing on this scale and not for the same reasons. But the thousands pouring into the wilderness after Anthony, and the millions through history since, did so because they were seeking virtue, mastery of self and peace with God. The same drive can be found in the Buddhist communities built deep in the Nepalese mountains, in the spirit walks of the Indigenous peoples of North America and in many other traditions.

When we are at war with ourselves, we are at war with the world around us as well. An unquiet, restless or tortured heart will not find rest or peace anywhere outside itself, even in the wilderness temples of God, until it is addressed directly. This requires courage and the willingness to see the truth about ourselves and our actions, and our impact on the world around us. "Acquire the Spirit of peace," Saint Seraphim of Sarov once said, "and thousands around you will be saved."[47] But the acquisition of peace is not a passive exercise; it requires discipline, endurance, self-sacrifice and humility. We cannot fall into the trap of thinking that just going on a few hikes, or even going off the grid altogether, will bring us the peace we seek or heal our fragmented relationship with the natural world.

The human being is in an undeniably unique position in the ecosystems of earth. No other animal or organism has the degree of impact on its environment that we do. We have the ability to transform the environment as much as to destroy it. It is a terrible responsibility, one we cannot avoid now that there are seven billion of us. The importance of careful stewardship of the earth has never been greater.

This is one of the primal messages in the garden

story of Genesis. In it, we are formed from the dust of the ground, not from the seed of a tree or a part of an animal, and certainly not as a descending spirit from God. Our origin is in soil, dirt, which is the womb of all life. The Latin word for soil is *humus*, from which we derive the word "humility." We trample it, plant in it, dig and move it and, these days, pollute it, rarely considering that without it life would not be possible. Yet it never ceases to provide for our needs. The idea that we are drawn from soil and return to it makes the human being more than in solidarity with it; we are a midwife to what it produces.

This is why we are told twice, before and after our disastrous encounter with the serpent, that we are "to cultivate and to keep ... the ground from which [we] are taken" (Gen. 2:15, 19). This is also why, in the story, breaking our union with God introduced such disharmony into the natural order. We turned from our friendship with the divine and became focused on our own needs and self. Our relationship to the environment reflects our relationship to ourselves, and ultimately to the creator. In other words, the wilderness we go into will flourish or fade depending on the wilderness we bring with us.

planetary ecosystem. We have stared down extinction before and survived just fine. True, this is the first time we may actually have had a hand in what climate scientists consider the Holocene extinction, or Sixth Extinction, event, but the jury is very much out on how much of it will be our own doing and how much is just a result of earth's ongoing shifts and changeability. We are not even sure if we have years or hundreds of years left. Regardless, the odds are that we will continue to flourish, even if we do so in ways unimaginable to us now. But we are kidding ourselves if we think there is a green utopia just around the corner. All the innovation and adaptive advantage in the world will do nothing to change the deeper issues at play.

A married couple once told me how they survived divorce. Things between them had become so bad that they had drawn up a separation agreement and already worked out who would get the house and where the kids would live. They decided to make one last attempt at counselling. The counsellor told them that if they did not address the deeper problems within themselves, they would both be back in her office a few years later with different partners. This changed everything for them;

they decided to take the counsellor at her word and found that their enmity really wasn't with each other but with unresolved pain in themselves.

I'm suggesting the same dynamic is at play in our relationship with the environment, which suggests that adapting is not enough. We can build new, resilient cities, figure out ways to feed our populations and find renewable, zero-waste energies to help insulate us from whatever changes we face in our environment. Yet we will come back to the same problems again and again unless something radical is introduced into the relationship between us and nature. This something is an altar.

When Noah emerged from the ark, his first act on the renewed earth, before the soil had brought forth any vegetation, was to build an altar and make a sacrifice. He took one of each clean animal and bird and sacrificed them as burnt offerings. It is hard today to imagine that this was not considered a barbaric practice. No one these days in North America goes to their temple bringing lambs or birds to have the animals' throats slit and then be burned! If they tried, they would likely be arrested for animal cruelty (despite the fact that we cut the throats of millions of animals daily so my senses, my health, food in my fridge, each member of my family, my job and so on. By the time I was done, I had reached out into the stars and back into the dawn of creation, placing at last my ultimate gratitude at the creator's feet. The mysterious effect this had on me was to help me realize that I was surrounded everywhere with gifts, and that I myself was one. In fact, giving thanks implies that a gift has been given. This exercise didn't always work, of course. Sometimes I was too down or too much in my head. In such cases, I would, as I described previously, go out into the backcountry so I could find some restoration in its natural rhythms, and the beauty I encountered there never failed to crack me open enough for some gratitude to emerge.

When we express thanksgiving we are also acknowledging a relationship. For instance, if we are grateful for food on our table, we are really recognizing the animal that gave itself for us, the farmer that raised it and the hands that prepared the meal. Because a relationship is implicit, we can't be thankful in isolation, and this is the first powerful effect thanksgiving has upon us: we realize that we are not alone. A heart cultivated with thankfulness communes with the whole universe, because everything is connected to something. But gratitude also says something about the quality of that relationship, in that it denotes a caring, even loving, relationship. The one who gives and expresses love, and the one saying thank you to acknowledge that love. In just this simple exchange, a bond of union is formed regardless of race, wealth, species or distance. Thanksgiving is the cure for isolation and the means for unity. I can be thankful for anything at any time; it is within my power to be so at all times.

When I am standing at my altar in the wilderness, giving thanks for all I see and know, I am not only capable of salvation and eternal joy myself, I am capable of actualizing it in the world around me. This is not a privilege given to any other created thing on earth; rather, all things depend on my doing so. But tied to the act of thanksgiving is a sacrifice that must be offered, because it is the embodiment of that exchange of love.

Sacrifice

The sacrifice at our altar must be none other than our own self. This is what makes it so hard to offer and also why it requires and expresses love. We all make sacrifices regularly in marriage, raising children and helping friends. These can sometimes be painful because they require us to deny our own needs and wishes for the benefit of another. But when we do so we are quite literally giving life to those we are sacrificing ourselves for. A sacrifice is an act of life; it is a direct engagement with another person or thing. We are saying, "You matter to me!" and because you do, I am going to be active rather than passive in our relationship. In this way, a sacrifice is an action of love wherein the action itself is an embodiment of that love.

I want to return to the story of Noah in order to explain what I mean here. In the nine generations after Adam, the world became overrun with wickedness. The children of murderous Cain multiplied, it is said, and nature began to suffer under their hands. Exploitation, pollution, murder, tyranny, slavery and recalcitrance filled the new cities and the knowledge of the creator began to be obscured. God had had enough. He instructed Noah to build an ark that was big enough to contain two of every animal and bird on earth. This is less remarkable to me than the fact that Noah did so with little knowledge as to why. Imagine a farmer in Saskatchewan being asked to build a boat the size of a football field and for it to take him over a 120 years to do so, involving his three sons, their wives and tremendous hardship. This was Noah's task.

This was also Noah's first sacrifice. But what is often overlooked in the story is that this sacrifice was one he made not just for God but for the natural world as well. In other words, Noah's extraordinary labours represent a fidelity to the environment as much as faithfulness to God. He is embodying in this work a love and stewardship for the earth that recapitulates that of the original intent for Adam and Eve. We must not gloss over the fact that this work really meant a lifetime of sacrifice for Noah. Felling massive trees, dragging logs from distant groves, hewing and planing wood into beams, devising tools and pulleys to shape and place them, mixing and applying the thick, dark pitch – these were his daily tasks, and although we are dealing with a mythic figure in this story, I still feel that the daily drudgery I would imagine it being is important because it highlights the extent of the sacrifice.

I also feel that Noah's sacrifice is the example

for our times. When he emerged from the ark and stood at the altar to offer thanksgiving, he stood at the beginning of a new world as a prototype for our relationship to the earth. After all, God didn't ask him to build a boat only for his family; he asked him for a vessel that would contain all of creation. Far from being an expression of anthropocentric self-importance, Noah's sacrifice, with its drudgery, sweat, blood, faithfulness and pain, was made for every living thing. Yes, he made an offering of thanksgiving on behalf of creation through the blood of the animals, but it was his own blood that built the ark and, using the wood from it, built the altar as well.

At Noah's altar we find our own. And like his, it requires a sacrifice of ourselves for the benefit of the wilderness we build it within. This sacrifice will never be any less than that asked of Noah – a lifetime's work offered in solidarity with and for nature, even when we can hardly see the reason for it and when, in our darker moments, the work itself seems futile. Yet, in just such a sacrifice, we are also saving ourselves. In doing what he did for creation, Noah preserved himself and his family as well. I believe that we are sustained by the very "freshness deep down things" that we are working so hard to protect, nurture and preserve. All the sacrifices I make for my daughters, for instance, are rewarded many times over by what these girls give to me. But I am doing them ultimately no good, and teaching them all the wrong lessons, when I seek only to provide for them while ignoring the natural world, which we depend upon for the very air we breathe and food we eat.

I believe the human heart is the altar of God, and that the wilderness temple is incomplete until we bring this altar to it. We may spend a lifetime of sacrifice building it, but in so doing we discover a world charged with the grandeur of God, revealing a cosmic unity and a continuous creative diversity. Beauty will provide the instructions, the dimensions and the materials for the altar and it will refresh us in the task. We will raise our own temples to reflect this beauty. We will give thanksgiving for all we see and all we know in the wilderness temple of our maker. At our heart's altar, built of the sacrifice of our ecological stewardship, we become a priest in whom and through whom the mysteries of heaven and earth meet and kiss and dance before the love that lit the stars.

POSTSCRIPT
Ho'oponopono

I lived for a year in Hawaii in 2011. My Big Island home was like a mother to me. Her crescent beaches smiled at me, her air fed me, her warmth and sun embraced me. In Hawaii, nature is nurture. We are as close to the elemental formation of life on earth there as we will ever get and life is so abundant in its nutrient-charged soil that it can be a nuisance. While it is not paradise, it is, as a friend there says, good practice for living in one. Embedded in Hawaiian culture is an important concept I would like to offer here as an essential tool in spiritual ecology for the healing of the human/nature divide. *Ho'oponopono* is a compound Hawaiian word that describes total reconciliation. *Pono* means good, love, peaceful, correct, complete, beautiful, harmonious and upright. The whole word denotes the practice of finding pono in ourselves, our family and our world. While there is no one standard ritual for gaining pono, it is possible to draw a general outline of the process from its general practice.

The first stage requires that we acknowledge that things are not pono. I believe this is a miraculous first step because it cannot be forced on anyone. Fear of change, anger at perceived wrongs, confusion born of pain and entrenched ways of life all stand in the way. I don't think blame or shame belongs anywhere in the environmental debates of our day. We are all responsible in some degree for how nature is mistreated. We are afraid of change, have gotten used to our way of life and are all alike in being swept away, as Matthew Arnold observes, "with confused alarms of struggle and flight."[49] This is a time when we are becoming globally aware of our environmental responsibilities, but it's still too early for any individual to know what to do about them. Yet, with a little bit of courage, we can still recognize that there is a problem and that it requires a change of heart to fix it. This is the first and mighty step to ecological pono.

The second stage in ho'oponopono is to agree to

listen to the pain of the other party. This includes a willingness to express our pain. This too is a miracle of sorts, since the act of listening makes us vulnerable to the other. When we listen, we become open to another person's pain and in doing so face our own part in it. The First Nations in Canada, for instance, have been trying to express the pain they suffer severely at the hands of colonial governments and their people. In isolated instances they have been able to do so, but for the most part they are still being stonewalled and thus denied this healing act by a society that does not know how to respond. My hope is that the plight of wildlife and ecosystems around the world, suffering directly at our hands, even to extinction, will be heard by all of us. But, again, we must begin in our own hearts to open ourselves to such voices. This is not an easy part of the process. If it took so long and so much bloodshed for the American people to recognize that an African was not a slave but a human being, then how much more difficult will it be to take the suffering of an animal seriously or even recognize that it has the ability to suffer at all. Getting to this part of the ho'oponopono process, however, is essential because we are then engaged with the honest offering, it can be quite revealing to both, as it can open up levels that neither party saw as belonging to the quarrel. Still, the act itself is powerful, since there can be no greater expression than this of a person's desire to find pono with the other. Both sides see the other taking ownership for their part and both sides have taken the penultimate step toward embracing resolution. This also means that both parties are stating that they will stop the wrongs they are committing. I think there is no shortage of such expressions in environmental communities. We know very well, for instance, that our meat does not come from grocery stores and wasn't born in shrink wrap on polystyrene foam. We also know that diamonds and gold are dug up using the backs of Third World institutionalized slaves. Ho'oponopono, however, requires that we state such things out loud and take ownership of them.

The final part of the ho'oponopono ritual is the greatest miracle of all: forgiveness. In the movie *The Mission*, the character played by Robert De Niro must make a harrowing journey through an Amazonian jungle, carrying around his neck the weapons and armour he used to enslave the people living there. When he arrives at the top of a dangerously high waterfall, he is met by the men and women who lost their children to his actions and he expects his throat to be cut in retribution. Instead, they cut the burden from his back and he collapses, weeping at their forgiveness. He is soon ushered into their community life and devotes himself to working with them as an equal. This is ho'oponopono. Both parties in this stage ask, without expectation, for forgiveness. If given, pono is achieved. Note, however, that pono first requires full participation in every step along the way: recognition of the problem, listening, meditation, confession and forgiveness.

Forgiveness is an action of the heart that is made possible through love. We imitate the divine most clearly in granting it. We also initiate a new era wherein the old things have passed away and a new stage of life can begin. Asking for forgiveness, however, makes it all possible. We are never freer than when we ask for it, since we are already fully aware of our wrongs, ready to change and have nothing to hide anymore. Whether we are forgiven or not, we are ourselves able to move on in self-knowledge, unshackled from the passions and hurt that gave rise to the conflict. This is why it is so powerful in a spiritually minded ecology for us to undergo the ho'oponopono process with nature itself. When we contend with the environment, we are really contending with its creator and, of course, ours. For this very reason, I believe that asking forgiveness of the natural world, after undertaking the full journey such a question requires to be authentic, is the requisite first step of spiritual ecology. Our journey into the wilderness temple where we will build our altar and make a sacrifice of thanksgiving begins here, with ho'oponopono.

NOTES

1. See Ellen Turner, "Dylan Thomas' Poetic Manifesto," *Taking Back Our Brave New World* (blog), May 31, 2012, accessed September 21, 2014, http://takingbackourbravenewworld.blogspot.ca/2012/05/dylan-thomas-poetic-manifesto.html.

2. Olga Michael lived in Alaska from 1916 to 1979. More information about Saint Olga Michael and her life can be found at *Orthodox Wiki*, accessed September 21, 2014, http://orthodoxwiki.org/Olga_Michael.

3. Eliot, "Little Gidding," V, accessed October 1, 2014, www.columbia.edu/itc/history/winter/w3206/edit/tseliotlittlegidding.html.

4. Ibid.

5. Ibid.

6. See C.S. Lewis, *The Four Loves*.

7. See Pavel Florensky, *The Pillar and Ground of the Truth*.

8. Chesterton, *Orthodoxy*, c. 7 "The Eternal Revolution," accessed September 21, 2014, www.ccel.org/ccel/chesterton/orthodoxy.x.html.

9 Keats, "On Looking into Chapman's Homer," lines 9–10, in *Selected Poetry*.

10 Rowthorn, *The Wisdom of John Muir*, 190.

11 Collier, *Three Against the Wilderness*, 13.

12 Schmemann, *The Journals of Father Alexander Schmemann, 1973–1983*, 3.

13 Tennyson, "In Memoriam A.H.H.," 56:15, in *Selected Poems*, 175.

14 Lewis, *Surprised by Joy*, 205; Newton, *The Correspondence of Isaac Newton*, vol. 1, 416.

15 Rowthorn, *The Wisdom of John Muir*, 18.

16 Saint Maximus the Confessor, *On the Cosmic Mystery of Jesus Christ*, 90.

17 Ibid.

18 Ibid.

19 Blake, "Auguries of Innocence," lines 1–4, in Michael Cox, ed., *The Concise Oxford Chronology of English Literature*, 289.

20 Blake, "Jerusalem," line 8, in Cox op. cit.

21 Hopkins, "God's Grandeur," in *The Poems of Gerard Manley Hopkins*, W.H. Gardner and N.H. MacKenzie, eds., 66.

22 Hopkins, *The Journals and Papers of Gerard Manley Hopkins*, Humphry House and Graham Storey, eds., 34.

23 de Saint-Exupéry, *The Little Prince*, c. 13.

24 Thomas, *The Poems of Dylan Thomas*, 9.

25 Basil of Caesarea, *On the Six Days of Creation: A Translation of the Hexaemeron by R. Grosseteste*, 2:7.

26 Sinkewicz, *Evagrius of Pontus*, 61.

27 See Molly Redden, "Whatever Happened to the Evangelical–Environmental Alliance?" *New Republic*, November 3, 2011, accessed September 21, 2014, www.newrepublic.com/article/politics/97007/evangelical-climate-initiative-creation-care.

28 "Creation care" is a term prominent among modern evangelical Protestants, used to describe an approach to ecology in which we are called to be stewards of creation according to a Biblical mandate to be so.

29 Rowthorn, *The Wisdom of John Muir*, 75.

30 Ibid., 92.

31 Wordsworth, "The World Is Too Much with Us," in Cox, *The Concise Oxford Chronology of English Literature*, 1802.

32 Dostoevsky, *The Idiot*, 382.

33 See "Alexandr Solzhenitsyn Nobel Lecture," Part 2, accessed September 21, 2014, www.nobelprize.org/nobel_prizes/literature/laureates/1970/solzhenitsyn-lecture.html.

34 Frankl, *Man's Search for Meaning*, 60.

35 Bartlett, *FlickWerk*, 13.

36 Cohen, *The Future*, track 5 (6:09).

37 These comprise a method of building walls whereby a mix-
    ture of earth is compacted in layers between forms.

38 See "Phos Hilaron," *Wikipedia*, accessed October 1, 2014,
    http://en.wikipedia.org/wiki/Phos_Hilaron.

39 See "El Castillo, Chichen Itza," *Wikipedia*, accessed
    September 21, 2014, http://en.wikipedia.org/wiki/
    El_Castillo,_Chichen_Itza.

40 Velimirović and Free Serbian Orthodox Diocese of the USA
    and Canada, *Prayers by the Lake*, lxxxix.

41 Rowthorn, *The Wisdom of John Muir*, 33, 34.

42 Ibid., 37–38.

43 Ibid., 35.

44 Thomas, "Fern Hill," in *The Poems of Dylan Thomas*, 16–17.

45 Athanasius, *The Life of Antony*, 77.

46 Ibid.

47 Rose, trans., *Little Russian Philokalia*, vol. 1: *St. Seraphim
    of Sarov*, 74.

48 Hobbes, *Leviathan*, J.C.A. Gaskin, ed., 13:9.

49 Arnold, "Dover Beach," line 36, in Christopher Ricks, ed.,
    The New Oxford Book of Victorian Verse, 304.

BOOKSHELF

Athanasius, Saint Patriarch of Alexandria. *The Life of Antony and the Letter to Marcellinus.* Translated by Robert C. Gregg. New York: Paulist Press, 1980.

Bartlett, Christy, James-Henry Holland and Charly Iten. *FlickWerk: The Aesthetics of Mended Japanese Ceramics.* Catalogue of exhibition at Johnson Museum of Art, Cornell University, Ithaca, NY, June 28 to August 10, 2008, and at Museum für Lackkunst, Münster, Germany, September 9 to October 12, 2008. Accessed July 14, 2014 (pdf) at www.bachmanneckenstein.com/downloads/Flickwerk_The_Aesthetics_of_Mended_Japanese_Ceramics.pdf.

Basil of Caesarea. *On the Six Days of Creation: A Translation of the Hexaemeron by R. Grosseteste.* Translated by C.F.J. Martin. Oxford: Oxford University Press, 1996.

Carrigan, Henry L. Jr., ed. *The Wisdom of the Desert Fathers and Mothers.* Brewster, Mass.: Paraclete Press, 2010.

Chesterton, G.K. *Orthodoxy.* New York: Dodd, Mead & Co., 1908.

Clements, Arthur L. *The Mystical Poetry of Thomas Traherne.* Cambridge, Mass.: Harvard University Press, 1969.

Cohen, Leonard. *The Future*. Columbia 4724982, 1992, CD.

Collier, Eric. *Three Against the Wilderness*. Victoria, BC: TouchWood Editions, 2007.

Cox, Michael, ed. *The Concise Oxford Chronology of English Literature*. Oxford: Oxford University Press, 2004.

Da Samraj, Adi. *The Spiritual Instructions of Saint Seraphim of Sarov: A Spirit-Baptizer in the Eastern Christian Tradition*. Clearlake, Calif.: Dawn Horse Press, 1991.

de Saint-Exupéry, Antoine. *The Little Prince*. Translated by Richard Howard. San Diego, Calif.: Harcourt, 2000.

Dostoevsky, Fyodor. *The Idiot*. Translated by Richard Pevear and Larissa Volokhonsky. New York: Alfred A. Knopf, 2002.

Eliot, T.S. *Collected Poems, 1909–1962*. New York: Harcourt, Brace & World, 1963.

————. *On Poetry and Poets*. London: Faber & Faber, 1957.

Florensky, Pavel. *The Pillar and Ground of the Truth: An Essay in Orthodox Theodicy in Twelve Letters*. Translated and annotated by Boris Jakim with an introduction by Richard F. Gustafson. Princeton, NJ: Princeton University Press, 2004.

Frankl, Viktor E. *Man's Search for Meaning*. Boston: Beacon Press, 2006.

Hobbes, Thomas. *Leviathan*. Edited by J.C.A. Gaskin. Oxford: Oxford University Press, 1998.

Hopkins, Gerard Manley. *The Journals and Papers of Gerard*

Manley Hopkins. Edited by Humphry House and Graham Storey. London: Oxford University Press, 1959.

———. *The Poems of Gerard Manley Hopkins*. Edited by W.H. Gardner and N.H. MacKenzie. 4th ed., based on 1st ed. of 1918 and enlarged to incorporate all known poems and fragments. London: Oxford University Press, 1970.

Jacobs, Jane. *Dark Age Ahead*. Toronto: Vintage Canada, 2005.

Keats, John. *Selected Poetry*. Oxford: Oxford University Press, 1998.

Lewis, C.S. *Surprised by Joy: The Shape of My Early Life*. New York: Harcourt Brace, 1955, 1995.

———. *The Four Loves*. New York: Harcourt, Brace, 1960.

Mander, Jerry. *Four Arguments for the Elimination of Television*. New York: Morrow, 1978.

New American Standard Bible. Nashville: Broadman & Holman, 1977.

Newton, Sir Isaac. *The Correspondence of Isaac Newton*. Vol. 1. Edited by H.W. Turnbull. Cambridge: Cambridge University Press, 2008.

Ricks, Christopher, ed. *The New Oxford Book of Victorian Verse*. Oxford: Oxford University Press, 1987.

Rilke, Rainer Maria. *The Selected Poetry of Rainer Maria Rilke*. Edited by Stephen Mitchell. New York: Random House, 1982.

Rose, Seraphim, trans. *Little Russian Philokalia*, vol. 1: *St.*

Seraphim of Sarov. Wildwood, Calif.: St. Xenia Skete Press, 1997.

Rowthorn, Anne W., ed. *The Wisdom of John Muir: 100+ Selections from the Letters, Journals and Essays of the Great Naturalist*. Birmingham, Ala.: Wilderness Press, 2012.

Saint Maximus the Confessor. *On the Cosmic Mystery of Jesus Christ*. Translated by Paul M. Blowers and Robert Louis Wilken. Crestwood, NY: St. Vladimir's Seminary Press, 2003.

Schmemann, Alexander. *For the Life of the World: Sacraments and Orthodoxy*. Crestwood, NY: St. Vladimir's Seminary Press, 1982.

———. *The Journals of Father Alexander Schmemann, 1973–1983*. Crestwood, NY: St. Vladimir's Seminary Press, 2000.

Sigrist, Seraphim. *Theology of Wonder*. Crestwood, NY: St. Vladimir's Seminary Press, 2001.

Sinkewicz, Robert E., trans. *Evagrius of Pontus: The Greek Ascetic Corpus*. Oxford: Oxford University Press, 2006. Accessed July 14, 2014 (preview only) http://site.ebrary.com/id/10177964.

Solzhenitsyn, Aleksandr. *The Solzhenitsyn Reader: New and Essential Writings, 1947–2005*. Edited by Edward E. Ericson Jr. and Daniel J. Mahoney. Wilmington, Del.: ISI Books, 2006.

Tennyson, Alfred. *Alfred Lord Tennyson: Selected Poems*. Edited by Aidan Day. New York: Penguin Books, 1991.

Thomas, Dylan. *Collected Poems, 1934–1952*. London: J.M. Dent & Sons, 1952.

———. *The Poems of Dylan Thomas*. Edited by Daniel Jones. Revised edition. New York: New Directions, 2003.

Velimirović, Nikolaj, and Free Serbian Orthodox Diocese of the USA and Canada. *Prayers by the Lake*. Grayslake, Ill.: Free Serbian Orthodox Diocese of the United States of America and Canada, 1989.

Wiesel, Elie, and Marion Wiesel. *Night*. New York: Hill and Wang, 2006.

ABOUT THE AUTHOR

Father Kaleeg Hainsworth is an author, speaker, poet, naturalist, podcaster and Eastern Orthodox priest. He has been writing and speaking for more than 20 years on subjects as diverse as poetics, literature, Christian history, Biblical exegesis, Eastern spiritual traditions, family structure, addiction therapy and ecology. He holds an honours BA in literature from the University of British Columbia and an MA in divinity from Saint Vladimir's Theological Seminary in New York. He founded and served an Orthodox parish in Victoria, BC, for ten years, during which time he established a youth camp and an outreach centre for the poor and also served as a chaplain at the University of Victoria. As an avid and respected naturalist, backcountry enthusiast and ecological educator, Father Hainsworth has led numerous guided trips into the British Columbia wilderness, where he has taught spiritual ecology, survival and team building to youth and adults alike. He resides in Vancouver, BC, with his three daughters, Ella, Heulwen and Bridget. This is his first book with RMB, the fruit of over 30 years of reflection and teaching on ecology and spirituality.

The RMB manifestos

PASSIONATE. PROVOCATIVE. POPULIST.

RMB has created one of the most unusual non-fiction series in Canadian publishing. The books in this collection are literary, critical and cultural studies that are meant to be provocative, passionate and populist in nature. The goal is to encourage debate and help facilitate positive change whenever and wherever possible. Books in this uniquely packaged hardcover series are limited to a length of 20,000–25,000 words. They're enlightening to read and attractive to hold.

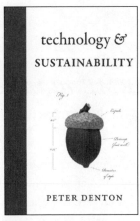

technology &
SUSTAINABILITY

PETER DENTON

ISBN 978-1-771600-39-2

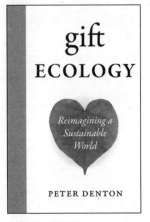

gift
ECOLOGY

*Reimagining a
Sustainable
World*

PETER DENTON

ISBN 978-1-927330-40-1

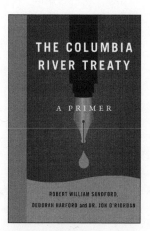

ISBN 978-1-771600-42-2

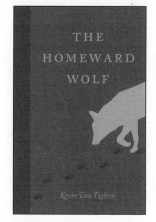

ISBN 978-1-927330-83-8

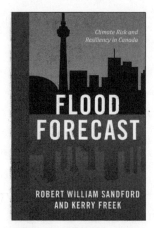

ISBN 978-1-771600-04-0

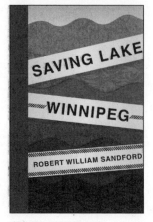

ISBN 978-1-927330-86-9

ISBN 978-1-926855-70-7

ISBN 978-1-897522-61-5

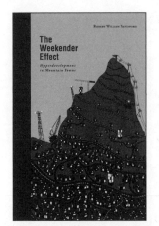

ISBN 978-1-897522-10-3

ISBN 978-1-926855-72-1

ISBN 978-1-927330-80-7

ISBN 978-1-926855-68-4

ISBN 978-1-926855-58-5

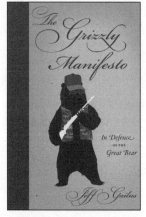

ISBN 978-1-897522-83-7

ISBN 978-1-926855-67-7

ISBN 978-1-926855-65-3

ISBN 978-1-927330-89-0

ISBN 978-1-927330-21-0

RMB saved the following resources by printing the pages of this book on chlorine-free paper made with 100% post-consumer waste:

Trees · 6, fully grown

Water · 2,760 gallons

Energy · 3 million BTUs

Solid Waste · 185 pounds

Greenhouse Gases · 509 pounds

CALCULATIONS BASED ON RESEARCH BY ENVIRONMENTAL DEFENSE AND THE PAPER TASK FORCE. MANUFACTURED AT FRIESENS CORPORATION.